# THE NEW WOMAN WARRIOR

The strength of a woman is a subtle thing. This strength need not show itself as physical force, commanding speech or aggressive behavior normally associated with power in this, a man's world. The force of a woman is a gentle undercurrent, seldom recognized, which lies in her perceptive and intuitive qualities, her sensitivity and her great joy in giving love and affection.

In today's world there is much conflict between the true nature of a woman and society's programmed image of her, whether she is an executive, homemaker, or both. This conflict can permeate all levels of a woman's life from how she wears her hair to how she handles herself in love, family and career relationships.

Join Marjorie Curtis in her warm and friendly kitchen as she entertains and touches you with her wisdom and observations on...

*Marriage*
"...the effort we made to remain in touch through those hardest years allowed us to eventually recognize that the dilemma was not a contest of Ron vs. Marge nor Male vs. Female, but the dilemma of Life. So instead of fighting to win battle after battle, we finally discovered that if we would join together we could win the war."

*Homemaking, Raising Children*
"For women to feel less because they work at home instead of out is one of the crimes of the decade.... There is that age-old myth that man envies woman for being the ultimate creator, producer of human beings.

The ultimate, as I see it is not the ability to produce them, but to raise them into healthy and whole young adults, and this takes all the tuning in, patience and love that it takes to be a Brancusi or a Matisse."

*Growing Young*
"We are not old and unattractive at thirty-eight as the media is so fond of telling us. Living where we are in the moment-by-moment gives us strength, and with strength comes beauty... I'm more myself than ever, healthier, clearer and rolling."

# The
# New
# Woman
# Warriors
# Handbook

NOT FOR
WOMEN ONLY

## Marjorie Curtis

## The New Woman Warriors Handbook
## Not for Women Only

Photo by Ron Curtis

PUBLISHING
P.O. Box 3100
Menlo Park, CA 94025 U.S.A.

This book is humbly and lovingly dedicated to all the ECK Masters, known and unknown, and especially to Sri Darwin Gross, The Living ECK Master of our time.

*Thanks to:* Hennie Slonim, Nancy Slonim Aronie, Betty Angell, Pat Yosha, Marilyn Nelson Warniak, Ann Curtis, Esther Katz, Ida Curtis, Carol Casiero, Judi Breit, Naomi Katz, Paulette Carter, Karen Tolczyk, Michael Beer, Danielle Hanrahan, Joan Roemer, Joyce Donahue, Cheryl Smith, Marti Berneike, Ruth Sessions, Sharon Dowaliby, Jennifer Colman, Laura Dowaliby, Beth Wilson, Valerie Wilson, Celeste Bancroft, Peter Brooks, Frances Blackwell, Gloria Hodgson, Joan Foberg and John Whitty as well as so many others that granted me interviews, opinions, experiences and time.

*Acknowledgements* to the mighty four whom I live and love with, Ron, Adam, Jenn and Elizabeth who were unfailingly supportive in this endeavor. A loving thanks to Paul Twitchell, Richard Bach, Joan Grant, Maxine Hong Kingston, Patti Simpson, Jean Weatherford Strong, Harold Klemp and Darwin Gross whose words of compassion, imagery, power, and wisdom have given me the courage to train the warrior within myself.

Twitchell: *The Flute of God*
Bach: *Illusions*
Grant: *The Winged Pharoah*
Kingston: *Woman Warrior*
Simpson: *Hello Friend*
Strong: *Testing Ground*
Klemp: *The Wind of Change*
Gross: *From Heaven to the Prairie*

# PURPOSE

To demonstrate the need to step out of bondage and the way to do it.

To bring about curiosity and desire to find out for one's self the reality we have allowed to be programmed out of us.

We are all warriors.

The word does not imply violence, but rather the war between ourselves and history, ourselves and society, and most of all, ourselves and ourselves.

# CONTENTS

# PROLOGUE

In my search for the answers to the unanswerable, I have read, listened to, and put myself in jeopardy with many different people. I have stumbled and fallen many times, but each time found me on a higher landing although it never appeared that way at the time. Only in retrospect could I see how the mistakes taught me, the suffering strengthened me and confidence came as a reward for coming through. Whenever I have been in the midst of a crisis, I could never see beyond to the lighter side, but some kind of "sonar" managed to lead me out. Time gives us some perspective and as we heal it gives us the courage to go forth. Sometimes the courage doesn't show itself, however, leaving us scared and emotionally paralyzed. These times can be called "rest times." We all need a break sometimes, and sometimes it takes a while before the water clears, leaving us free once again to act. The important thing at these times is to let ourselves be. Not to push and judge, because some of the best work gets done when we are seemingly standing still.

There are things between these pages that will be frightening to some and absurd to others. For a few it will come as a relief and the beginning of a joyous change as it was for me when I came upon much of this information which I had to prove for myself. In a way I am pointing out some of the milestones in my personal journey with the knowledge that some of these milestones may look like some of yours.

The book has been written because it appeared to me in the dream state with the title and format as they are. I gratefully accepted it as an assignment. Although *The New Woman Warriors Handbook* is based on my own experiences and that of others whom I've come across in my search, I can only say

xiii

that most of the time I was only the holder of the pen. The book has happened because of those of you whose lives it will change. Many parts of this spiritual journey are intensely physical and emotional and yet there is not one moment in all of life that is not spiritual once we begin to become aware of the big picture. Here is a handbook to guide you through your own journey and an alarm clock to wake up the warrior within you so you can emerge victorious in the battle of life.

## Author's Note

Karma—Karma is the law of cause and effect, action and reaction, it is the law of You Reap What You Sow.

The working out of karma takes place over many lifetimes so that in the long run there is total justice for all. It is definitely not a law of crime and punishment but rather a perfect balancing out of negative and positive action over a period of time. Nothing is free. You have either earned it or will pay for it. No suffering is without reason, you have either earned it or will be compensated for it. There is no blame, we are the result of our own consciousness, we are responsible for everything we do and no one can take that responsibility for us. We do well to develop our own awareness so that we move in a state of consciousness from being effect to becoming cause.

chapter one

# BACK TO BIRTH
## Becoming a Person

It begins when we choose to be born. Actually it begins way before that, but for the sake of "now" let's start with what is familiar, a new beginning into a physical existence as a brand new baby...

In reality, we do exist long before we come into that brand new baby body. We, meaning the important part of ourselves, the very highest part, higher than the body, higher than the mind, the part of ourselves we call Soul.

I know, we usually think of ourselves as "having a soul" or maybe our soul goes to heaven when we die, but that's not really how it works. What really happens is that our soul has us. Or rather we, as Soul, have a body; a female one or a male one, whichever we (as Soul) decided on for this particular dance—this particular lifetime. Yes, we choose the whole situation we come into; our parents, the kind of environment, body type, the whole thing. We don't really choose an easy life or one that would be fun and famous necessarily. We choose what we as Soul need to experience this time round, what we're willing to put ourselves through in order to eventually reach perfection. It has to do with karma, which we will get to later.

If you're still with me, good. It'll get clearer the more we go along. Some of the questions you have been asking yourself about existence and identity have simple answers but take time to explain.

Let's assume for now that we have been around for as long as we care to remember, perhaps millions and millions of years—we, the eternal part of ourselves having taken on numerous bodies, have had some very amazing adventures. In the beginning, the real beginning, we were created, as Soul; a tiny atom of awareness which took on many different and progressively advancing physical forms. We lived, an ever growing consciousness, an ever unfolding being in the physical bodies of the worlds, the elements, the rocks, the vegetables, the animals and finally into human baby form.

Now we begin our series of human adventures. Much that we thought of as history we carry in Soul memory right within us. From this point on we dance to many different tunes, fight in many different wars, wear the crowns of royalty perhaps, and the hats of authority, the tattered shoes of peasants and the shoelessness of slaves. We carry ourselves through the ages within the bodies of many races, both sexes, the beautiful and the ugly, the weak and the fit, all to experience what it is to be "that." All for the education of Soul.

Now you are holding this book in your hands, and your consciousness, through an endless rotation of experiences has risen to the point of wonder—the faintest glimmer of a memory about this cycle of infinite lifetimes as a possibility of truth, whether consciously or unconsciously, you, as a separate entity from all the rest, have within you the stored records of your past. It is not my intent to help you find your pasts' most treacherous or glamourous moments, but it is my intent to provide a possible key to unlock your own potential to all knowingness about yourself.

Pandora's Box or a treasure of sacred truth? It's up to you.

This book is being written to those of you who, like myself, have become reckless in the search for truth, for those of you who have discovered within, a point of carefully hidden weariness, a lack of peace, for those of you who know there is something yet unseen but close to the edge here, for those of you who have spent a millenium traipsing through lifetimes rising ever higher toward your true self and now finally want to know why, for those many of you who keep asking "Who am I? Where am I going?" In my research, I have found those answers...for me. My goal now is to give you a set of keys, one of which if you really want it to, will unlock the door to the answers that lie right within yourself.

## BACK TO BEING BORN

You are born. Here you come, a beautiful, innocent helpless little baby. You have a brand new body and a brand new mind. Into your birth you brought with you a deep, deep memory of your past, but for your survival it will begin to disappear so as not to interfere with your new life. Into your new life you also brought with that memory a lot of excess baggage, some of your most clinging hangups. Into this new life you brought with you yourSELF, the SOUL you've always been. In the meantime, having spent a lot of time without this new and helpless body, you still know how to get along without it, so as a little baby you spend much of your time wandering happily, learning from journeying into the infinite other worlds and planes as we sometimes call them. People see you sleeping, peaceful and soft, having no idea you're not even in there. Not knowing you are drifting far away, enjoying other places, adventures and even relationships. You are free and can go anywhere without the encumberance of a helpless and confining body. Sometimes you begin to cry or even scream when you have to return to your prison in the physical world. Still you are wise, for your reality is not limited at all. As you grow and learn to communicate, to learn love and behavior from your parents and later your teachers, your wisdom begins to be replaced by a new set of standards—standards as limiting as your physical body—and you are on your way to becoming a person.

# STARSCAPE BABY VISION: Night Journey two

i
drawn upward on currents past the moon,
I hover above my crib then whisk upward thru the window
                                            rise
                    I
              as
         and
I grow in memory and
   strength of recollection...
        "I must go home"
           but where is home? I do not know
              and vaguely
                    look
                       down
                          to the house where
                          my body resides,
                             and sigh.


ii
once yet again am I in baby form...
helpless...dependent...who to understand that I am NOT what i seem to be


iii
                 upward to the Moon,
      then I flee              she, both form in the quiet
and                           music of the sky and a
                                      sentient entity.
iv
gently I greet her and
am embraced by her recognitions,
once I had taken form and dwelled on her
                          three-dimensioned sphere,
but that was long ago and now am many dimensions
                       knowingness beyond...
as we share the joke that those who travel
between time bands
                know about.

v

I smile
and it is forgotten that
my current binding form
is baby yet.....for I
    have yet another form for Here and
    many many forms of Consciousness for
               There,
                    or there,
but most beautiful jest of all
is that my REAL self
        is no-Thing at all
            but NOW  (No body-transient,
                        tacit agreement of
                        atomic chemistry easily
                        displaced on the plasma tides
                        of time and space, though
                            I survive)[1]

---

[1]Anya Graber Foos, *Skycleaver* (Connecticut: 1975), p. 13.

The day my thighs got slim
I put on a tiny striped shirt and someone's
    smaller jeans
And with the sun shining and a lot of skin
    showing
I could find no one I know

*Levels of Understanding*
Knowing what it is to drive a Ford
Knowing what it is to drive a Ferra
What is a car?
What is health?
What is your level of understanding

## chapter two

# IT'S ONLY YOUR BODY FOR NOW
## Health, Sex and Reincarnation

AS A KID I HAD A HARD TIME WALKING FROM ONE TELEPHONE POLE TO THE NEXT. As a twelve-year old, I lied to my friends and told them I had a bad heart because although the doctors didn't think there was anything wrong with me, my body still refused to behave. I used to wish I had a name for my invisible handicap, and as a teenager when guys used to ask me out, I'd spend the whole week worrying how far away he would park and almost envying people in wheel chairs who knew why they couldn't walk and whom nobody expected anything from. Guilt, pain and shame from having such thoughts. Through the years, I realized that I wasn't so bad by myself, but as soon as I was with anyone or had to rush somewhere, I'd stop breathing, and pain, nausea and paralysis would set in, to say nothing of the humiliation and self-hate. It felt as if I were a robot and the battery in my legs had died, leaving me with heavy metal locked in place. Sometimes I'd stop and window shop just so I could sneak a rest, pretending to be fascinated by a stack of Pyrex bowls in a hardware store window.

At school I was the last one picked for teams. I wasn't picked. I was left over. In high school, I got my period every week to get out of gym. She let me. I wish that someone could have shown me ways of pushing through at that early age. For one thing I always thought that there are natural-born athletes and if it hurt, you weren't one. A yogi said, "No pain, no gain." I say, "So who knew?"

I was lucky because I looked O.K., but unlucky because everyone expected me to be able to do things.

It was hard for me to play and I never ever competed as it would only reinforce failure. So I missed out on a lot of what looked like fun.

> My dream was to be a ballet dancer
> but I didn't know that dreams could come
>     true
> So I didn't work hard enough
> I thought
> you woke up one day in pale pink leotards
> and pirouetted to the bathroom
> looked into the mirror and saw a dancer
>     there.
>
> I waited and slept and nothing happened
> Oh, I took lessons but
> The toe shoes really hurt
> and the stretches made my hamstrings ache.
>
> I slept some more hoping the dream
> would soon release me from the pain
> But I was young
> and really dumb
> and I never met a person
> who said they had a dream
>
> So I slept
> and dreamed
> and wished
> and wondered when
> I'd wake up dancing.[1]

[1]Nancy Slonim Aronie (Connecticut: 1981).

At thirty-eight I decided I'd atrophy soon from inactivity if I didn't put myself into some kind of program that would force me to break through this mystery. My friend Pat convinced me to call a local Reality Therapist and make an appointment. It was a giant step. I finally admitted that I had a problem I couldn't solve on my own and dialed the number. After about six sessions, I seemed ready to tackle a group situation, actually joining a swimming class, diving off the deep end and passing the Red Cross test. That little white card gave me the courage to take the next step.

I thought Tai Chi being a very slow and unhurried form of exercise, would be a good place to start. Much to my amazement, I eventually found myself among actual Kung Fu practitioners also studying there. They terrified me with their violent moves, but because of the understanding and the compassion of the people, I was able to spend several years studying martial arts under that roof.

In order to even stand in line in the silent beginnings of that class which always began with a brief meditation, I had the chance to mentally fortify myself by saying over and over again, "I don't care what anyone thinks. This is for me and my survival." I later discovered that many of the guys in my class were struggling just as hard against their own odds. This is when the word warrior began to be a concept. It emerged from physical agony and despair to extreme pride and elation; bursting through barriers and penetrating beyond my physical and emotional self. My thirty-eight year old body began to show signs of tone and my physical confidence began to build. To this day, I'm not sure what caused the immobility as a very young child, but I do know that with each passing year, as more and more confidence was lost, the body had become more and more conditioned to immobility with the exception of two things—sex and dancing, and I guess that was because I was able to lose myself to music and to love. Perhaps the same could be said about practicing body postures, breath control and mental concentration in Hatha Yoga, although the disciplines are quite different.

For those of you in good shape or who prefer to jog, etc., definitely check out some Warm Up Stretching Exercises before beginning your workout for more endurance and less pain. The Martial Arts from the east; Kung Fu and Tai Chi from China; Karate, Aikido and Judo from Japan; Tae Kwon Do from Korea and Okinawan Karate have swept this country with enormous popularity. Because of the current fad, these ancient traditions are being bastardized by opportunists. Degrees are awarded and masters are made for economic and prestige purposes. If the martial arts interest you, be sure that when you look for your teacher, you do some shopping around. Don't get caught in somebody's ego trip or self-made dogma. You will know what's right for you by the feeling you get. Then go for it!

When I was in Taipei, we went into a park at dawn and it was July. Old people were practicing their forms in the shade of ancient trees—what appeared to be very old men and women and many younger and very young people as well. It was silent and golden, full of grace.

Tai Chi and Kung Fu are one way to approach this. There are many ways to do so. For me, my body got stronger, but the mystery still wasn't solved. Hills and stairs still threatened me with anxiety, particularly under pressure, but the discipline of the art gave me strength in between.

"Tai Chi is a subtle and powerful awareness discipline, a tool to become more in touch with yourself. It is a way of allowing yourself to function naturally and smoothly, uncluttered with expectations, "shoulds," hopes, fears and other fantasies that interfere with our natural flow."[2]

Now I work out at Gloria Stevens for an hour every day, not as dramatic as Kung Fu, but the most unjudgemental woman's place I have ever experienced. A place where all ages, races and sizes co-exist. I mean you can't help fitting in. There are athletes and dancers and great-grandmothers too, and tights and leotards show every puff of the body, but no one cares, you feel like working out and that counts. They call it a figure salon. Although it radically improves the figure, it is designed for the health of the heart and lungs as well as all the other parts that don't show in a bathing suit.

Whatever age we are, whatever month it is, Now is the time for taking responsibility for educating ourselves and our children, concerning such things as the dangers of being a "civilized woman/person." Consider the American diet if you are ready to take a look at that. I wasn't, until just a few months ago when I finally made another step in getting my bodily act together. Now I've begun to eat better. I'm discovering just as what you eat is important it is also the amounts and the way you combine foods that determines health. It's still not perfect for me, but on its way, and since I've accepted working out as a pleasure in my life instead of a pain, for the first time I feel vital—and I'm fitting into my kids' clothes as a bonus.

---

[2]Al Chung-liang Huang, *Embrace Tiger, Return to Mountain,* intro. Barry and John Stevens (Utah: 1973), p. 7.

# FOOD COMBINATION CHART[3]

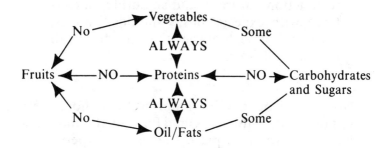

## VEGETARIANISM
From *Does it Matter?* by Alan Watts[4]
"Vegetarianism, for example, is no solution.
Years ago the Indian botanist, Sir Jagadis
Bose, measured the pain reactions of plants
to cutting and pulling. To say that plants
don't really know they are in pain is only to
say that they can't put it into words. When I
pointed this out to a strictly vegetarian
Buddhist, the famous Reginald H. Blyth,
who wrote Zen in English Literature, he
said, 'Yes, I know that. But when we kill
vegetables they don't scream so loud.' In
other words, he was just being easy on his
own feelings. Buddhist and Hindu monks
have carried the attitude of ahimsa or harm-
lessness, to the extreme of keeping their eyes
on the ground when walking—not to avoid
the temptation of lovely women, but to
avoid trampling beetles, snails, or worms
that might lie in the path. Yet this is at root
an invasion, a ritual gesture of reverence for
life which in no way alters the fact we live by
killing."

---

[3]Dr. Herbert Shelton, *Food Combining Made Easy.*
[4]Alan Watts, *Does it Matter?* (New York: 1971), p. 27.

Here is an example of the importance of getting oxygen into the body. The best way to do that is through exercise. Then the desire for carbohydrates decreases. In his book, besides showing the benefits of herbs and proper diet, Paul Twitchell gets into detail about people who fall into many categories and their combinations (hydrogen, nitrogen, magnesium, etc.).

"The next type is the carbon category. They are usually fleshy in body and spend most of their lives trying to get out of work. Because they are indisposed to work, they become inactive and retiring, lacking fire because they have upset the chemical balance of their bodies by too many sweets and starches. This type is usually overweight and babyish looking. If the individual cannot burn off the carbon in the body properly, he feels weak most of the time. The greater consumption of carbon, the greater the need for oxygen. Unless there is proper diet and sufficient exercise, they become lethargic and weak."[5]

## DANGERS OF BEING A CIVILIZED WOMAN/PERSON

Deodorant tampons and antiperspirant sprays shouldn't even have to be mentioned here. Again, since the government won't protect us from such dangers, we have to start thinking about protecting ourselves by reading labels, doing research and not trusting the experts.

## MENSTRUATION

Many of us burst into lustful cravings for ice cream, pastries and the great Milky Way. It is then that our

---

[5]Paul Twitchell, *Herbs, the Magic Healers* (California: 1971).

diets usually plummet to the bottom. This happens as a result of a drop in blood sugar which comes right before menstruation. Some licorice root could solve the problem, and is a way to restore balance.

*Toxic Shock Syndrome*
Some things to remember when using tampons.
1. Avoid leaving a tampon in place for longer than four hours since foreign material will encourage the growth of progressively greater numbers of microorganisms the longer it remains in the body.
2. Tampons with plastic applicators should not be used as they may scratch the vaginal lining, creating entry sites for bacteria. When menstrual flow is light, switch to sanitary napkins or mini-pads. Reason: during "light" days, a tampon is more apt to dry which may cause tiny tears in the vaginal lining during removal. Also, the tampon may shred, leaving small pieces of cotton in the vagina which may harbor bacteria.[6]

I was thinking about the positive side of menstruation. I think what happens with us is that because our bodies are in constant change throughout each cycle, one cycle leading into the next, it gets us used to enduring instability which also strengthens us emotionally, and provides us with a great deal of flexibility. Change is a challenge; a challenge to growth, and the negative part of menstruation and menopause and all the things we go through physically and emotionally can usually be greatly modified by taking nutritional supplements and herbs.

---

[6]Suggestions by: Drs. Michael Truppin and Alvin Berman, Obstetricians-Gynecologists affiliated with Mt. Sinai Hospital in New York City, *Harpers Bazaar,* March 1981, p. 84.

# DRUGS

It has been proven that drugs including marijuana puncture holes in the aura. Through Kirlian photography, we can see this damage.

> "The aura is the magnetic field which surrounds a person, composed of an emanative sphere of thought forces and emotions collected around the physical frame in the form of fine vibratory waves or rays of color."[7]

When a person is on drugs it can be seen through the Kirlian photograph that there are holes, spaces and irregularities around this protective force field that is a part of each of us. When there is an opening, negativity will be attracted to us in much the same way that an open wound attracts infection. We become vulnerable to depression, anger, fear, cravings, lack of energy and the most subtle form of negativity, illusion, thinking we are gaining something from the drug when in actuality we are hurting ourselves. Be careful.

# SEX

Don't worry about your sex life. Life in the supermarket line can send you into the pits if you let it. Bad enough you have to weed through aisles and aisles of chemical foods and pay through the nose for them, but while waiting to make the exchange your gaze inevitably falls on photographs of semi-clothed airbrushed bodies beckoning you to buy so you too can look as sexy, become a good sex partner and learn to have multiple orgasms as well. We're all familiar with the literature waiting for us at the end of the line and after we've already thrown a gallon of ice cream into the cart to boot.

---

[7]Paul Twitchell, *ECKANKAR Dictionary* (California: 1973).

All of this emphasis on normalizing your sexual self through articles and therapy, except for a few cases, is unnatural and abnormal. It is a gross form of manipulation.

Yes, I too have been known to take the quizzes and spend time working through a two page chart to find where I stack up in the national average. How can we let public pressure and the distorted emphasis on such a natural and personal act formulate our individual standards?

There are two things to remember when trying to understand our sexual identity. One is that when we have sexual intercourse with another we automatically exchange Karma with that person. We become more involved and more affected and effective with that person than we know. Even if we never see that person again we are left with an effect of taking on the Karma of that individual, or simply stated, taking on some of that person's cosmic debts.

The other thing is that if you happen to be one of many whose sexual desire level is low, it could very easily be that you've had more than your fill of sex in the past, in this lifetime or another. So, again, be true to yourself and try to communicate your needs and lack thereof to yourself and your partner.

To help avoid rape, walk brisk, confident and alert.


### Sun Bath

Hot rays on flesh are penetrating
reaching troubled, tangled
gut of woman, torn and troubled,

healing her. I bake here
like unleavened bread. Surprised

that one can parch for heat I
nurse at mother sun this spring.
My skin devours light like optimism.

A swollen seed, my heart sends shoots.
I shall rise in time like bread—
leavened, brown and sweet.[8]

## REINCARNATION

By reincarnation I don't mean returning to life in the form of a bat or an oyster or even a sunflower. What I'm talking about as mentioned before is a progression through lifetimes to continually higher states of consciousness. Since we are already human beings, we will most likely return again as human beings, but in a higher state of consciousness and with new things to experience. The cycle will continue until we're done experiencing all there is to experience, learning all there is for us to learn and until all of our debts are paid.

We will have already experienced "perfect" bodies in beauty and strength and its opposite, although probably for most of us, most of our bodies will be in between the extremes. This is all for the purpose of educating us. It's part of the big plan in expanding our consciousness so that we can understand and have compassion for everyone, having been like everyone else at one time or other. Through this process of being like everyone as we return again and again through birth and death, we retain our individuality as Soul, our true identity which is in itself immortal. It is the essence of our continuous individuality, the essence of our God selves. It's been said that "truth is stranger than fiction," and for many this is a tough one to swallow because of the various social hierarchies that exist. We in our human consciousness always have to know that we're better than someone else, and therefore, prejudice exists. So how can prejudiced persons accept such a concept that he/she was once black, white, red or yellow, a midget, obese,

---

[8]Joan Shapiro, *Coloring Book* (Connecticut: 1978), p. 79.

scarred, bald, birthmarked or burned? We protect ourselves from having to relate to all kinds of people by putting ourselves in a separate category, but the more we do that, the more we have to return into the form of that which we are putting down until we finally learn that we are all the same in that we are all Soul, which has no sex or color, no poverty or riches. We are only individuals putting on different outfits through different lifetimes. So, in essence, it really makes more sense to say, "I have a body" rather than "I have a Soul."

There is an article in *Psychology Today* citing a Gallup Poll which revealed that approximately 70% of the people in the United States believe in the hereafter. From that same article:

> "The time is 1978. The California Museum of Science and Industry opens an exhibit organized around the thesis that energy is indestructible, that consciousness can exist independent of the physical body, and that there is much evidence that consciousness continues after death. Designated "Continuum" the exhibit stresses the words of great philosophers who have supported the belief in life after death."

On page 66 the article goes on to say:
> "Most researchers do not appear to be 'cranks' who rationalize their interpretations with strong religious convictions, unjust attacks upon opposing viewpoints or complex neologisms. A rare few compare themselves with Einstein, Columbus, or Galileo in respect to the unconventional investigation of sacred scientific doctrine. But unlike the pseudoscientists described by mathematician Martin Gardner, who manifest strong

compulsions to attack the greatest scientists and best established theories, many current investigators of life after death try to accommodate their interpretations to establish scientific thinking."[9]

This, to me, is indeed admirable and a monumental task, for in my perception, when a person is ready to look beyond scientific thinking, they will see beyond scientific thinking. Science, after all, is merely a method of proof and measurement limited to the tools of the physical world. There is much we know today to be possible and true that science a century ago refused to consider. When we speak of science we speak of a field, but that field is made up of individuals. It is the imagination of the free thinking that can bring science into new dimensions, and then science in turn brings it to us. My question is, when we have our own imagination, which is only a step to wonder, and wonder is what leads us into discovery of truth, why wait for someone else to do it for us?

70% of the people in the United States believe in a hereafter, and yet we live a lifestyle contrary to our beliefs; we work and play in a "You only go round once" culture, without accepting the responsibility for our lives. If we agree with a theory we are obliged to explore its full meaning. We can't just say "Sure, I believe in reincarnation" and leave it at that. We have to understand what that means to us from moment to moment and then remember what we believe when a crisis comes. It is a temporary situation, something to go through to learn greater perspective from, and possibly, an opportunity to pay off a Karmic debt. We have more fun out of life when we realize it is one of many and there is a purpose for it all, and yet we

---

[9]Ronald K. Siegel, *Accounting for Afterlife Experiences* (New York: 1981).

(as a civilization) avoid the understanding of the true meaning of reincarnation and its Karmic implications.

We ask how this can happen to us and truly think we don't deserve the hardships handed us. Well, how can we ever know what we deserve if we can't remember our past? The trick is not to keep incurring debts and not to overdraw our account. For every action there is a reaction and we alone must find the balance. There is no hell as the religions speak of to punish us. There is no punishment. There is only karma which always catches up to us sooner or later, in a most exacting way. This is why we must learn to forgive others and very importantly, ourselves. Why do an anger number on ourselves? Why compound it with hatred toward ourselves or others when it will be taken care of by the Spiritual hierarchy, those beings beyond our realm of physical existence who work very closely under God, and who see to it that justice is done.

## To Merle

Say skinny many sided tall on the ball
brown downtown woman
last time i saw you was on the corner of
pyramid and sphinx
ten thousand years have interrupted our
conversation
but i have kept most of my words
till you came back.
What i'm trying to say is
i recognize your language and
let me call you sister, sister,
I been waiting for you.[10]

---

[10]Lucille Clifton, *Two Headed Woman* (Massachusetts: 1980).

I'm beginning to suspect the reason the whole idea of reincarnation is such a threatening concept, and even though we may believe in it when asked on a Gallup Poll, it is something that sits far in the background of our lives. I really think that the implication of living a life in awareness of returning to another life, and another implies taking on a lot more responsibility than most of us are willing to do. If indeed we do return to new bodies again and again, how then can we get away with as much as we think we are getting away with? The answer is we can't. It is this responsibility, and these very often heavy experiences we need to go through in working our way up to Self-realization or what we sometimes call Soul-realization. All of us are doing this whether we know it or not, whether we like it or not. It has nothing to do with religion. Soul is bent on getting home, back to the heavenly worlds from where it originated, back to the Godhead. Most of the way, we (as our lower selves) pull and tug the whole way back. Well, not the whole way or we'd never get there, but most of the way, just like a little kid who sits down in the middle of a cold, damp sidewalk crying from being tired, while "mommy" is trying to get her home where it's cozy and warm. Soul is like our "mommy" who wants to take care of us; who, if we listen, will take us back home again, where we'd rather be.

Many of us resist being here in the same way many of us resist going "home." During the process of writing to you, my big walking mystery got solved. After 43 years, it cracked wide open. It has to do with escape.

## ESCAPES

I discovered that it was not that energy wasn't going to my "iron-locked" legs, but simply a matter of my trying to get out, to avoid the tension or pressure of a situation. I wanted out but my old methods, my baby methods of leaving the body didn't work so good anymore, and I got trapped partially in, partially out. My poor legs didn't know what was going on. They just simply came to a halt. And my mind, of course, was confused, leaving me in most cases frustrated and humiliated. It was also my karma for the pain to take that form.

Now that I understand this, the situation is easier but not gone. As for my legs, I just shake them, talk to them, get flabbergasted that something is making me want to leave the situation, take a look at the situation, deal with the situation and everything is O.K. It's not perfect yet because I'm functioning off a lifetime habit. I have to retrain myself, de-program and re-program constantly, but now that I'm ready to handle this, the information came and I don't have to study Pyrex bowls in store windows much any more.

Many, many people do similar things. They invent their own methods of escape as young children or adolescents. Whatever works, keeping them from facing what they don't want to face, and yet accepting the pain and embarrassment of the alternative.

I'm convinced that epilepsy, autism, coma and crib death are some of the ways out, some more extreme than others.

The pain and guilt felt by the families and friends of these individuals would never be so severe if they understood about the continuity of life. Life after life after life, wave after wave after wave. The karma between all the individuals involved could be resolved in this act which could be the reason for it in the first place.

If you can accept this possibility, you will understand many things about life and death. One being that some women should not have children. They've done it before and learned it and need now to travel other roads in this incarnation. So, if that's how you feel, don't let potential grandparents or peer pressure get you pregnant.

We are not victims. None of us. We all choose from the highest part of ourselves what we need to experience and when, how we will work through our karma and when.

The physical body is only a clay shell, empty and dead without Soul. The body is the vehicle we use to gain experience in the physical world, so we might as well use it, have fun with it, keep it clean, strong and healthy. It's the only one we have for this lifetime. It's only your body for now!

## READING LIST

*Endocrines, Organs and Their Impact*
Edward F. Schwarz, Ph.D.
Edman Printing

*Herbs, the Magic Healers*
Paul Twitchell
IWP Publishing

*Everywoman's Book to Holistic Health*
Paavo Airola
Health Plus

*How to Get Well*
Paavo Airola
Health Plus

*Women and the Crisis in Sex Hormones*
Barbara Seaman & Gideon Seaman, M.D.
McClelland & Stewart Ltd.

*The People's Pharmacy*
Joe Graedon
Avon

*Nutrition Almanac*
Nutrition Search Inc.
McGraw Hill

*Childbirth Without Fear*
Dick Grantly Read

*Painless Childbirth*
Fernand LaMaze

*The Gentle Birth Book*
Nancy Berezin
Simon & Schuster

*The Rights of the Pregnant Parent*
Valmai House Elkins
Schocken Books, New York

*Birth Without Violence*
Frederick LaBoyer
Alfred A. Knoph

*So Your Happily Ever After Isn't*
Rocky Mountain Planned Parenthood

"The religious orders are attempting to convince not only all women, but the government as well, that the unborn child is a person. This is not so. The fetus is a biological entity only. The whole point is that Soul, which is that individual spark of God, does not enter the body while it is in the womb of the female, but only *after* the child has been brought into the outer world, and sometimes later than that.

Therefore, it is not murder if the woman decides not to bear the child and carry the responsibilities of feeding it, seeing it through school and out into life, any more than it is murder if I cut off a bit of skin from my finger. It is her decision alone; there is no Karma attached. There is nothing but the guilt and fear that has been pressed upon her through man's ignorance."[1]

---

[1] Darwin Gross, *Your Right to Know* (California: 1979), p. 37.

## chapter three
# ABORTION
## Experience With Soul

They are trying to take abortion away from us. That scares me because it takes freedom of personal choice away.

Those trying to illegalize abortion are many of the same people who storm into Planned Parenthood Centers on a daily basis, adament about the availability of education and contraception to teen-agers. The thing to be remembered here is that those providing the services are not condoning the sexual behavior of teen-agers. They are merely acting as instruments in protecting the lives of these young women as well as their unborn children.

The real tragedy is the young women who do not use contraception or abortion because of lack of responsibility, or guilt, or the desperate need for love and the desire to be needed. A child rearing a child is usually a lonely and grim event, often compounded by the indignities of being on welfare. If people are going to complain as taxpayers against abortion, let them look at the total picture.*

When I discovered I was pregnant for the fourth time, my kids were semi-grown and I could taste the coming freedom.

With one foot on the shelf and the rest of me draped warm and limply over the wood stove, stirring something in a pot, I can't remember what, I made a sudden decision that I really, in actuality, was indeed pregnant. This sleepiness and sudden interest in new

_____
*See reading list. Contraception, pregnancy, childbirth and hormonal problems are topics that are covered surprisingly and adequately in the books mentioned at the end of chapter two.

foods was all too familiar. I got dressed, borrowed some money and jumped on the next Greyhound to New York.

After the abortion I had some strange experiences. I'd be lying in bed at night about to doze off when I'd become aware of a presence. It felt sweet, loving and tender. It was clear to me that it was the entity of my unborn baby. At that time I didn't really understand what a fetus actually was and what an abortion actually did, but this entity seemed to be very forgiving and even appreciative somehow. We'd briefly exchange some love and then the presence would be gone. Comforted, I'd drop off to sleep. This occurred on several occasions, convincing me that my decision to have an abortion had been right, not only for myself but for this which might have been my baby. I never mentioned it until about the fifth time I was visited, and then I told Ron about it. He told me the same thing had been happening with him. We were both amazed but felt somehow blessed and it never again happened, but we were left guiltless and free.

Now that I know that Soul does not enter the baby body until it's out of the mother's womb I understand what happened. That Soul that would have entered my baby had I continued the pregnancy needed the experience with us and we needed the experience with it. There was some communication exchange that had to get done between the three of us. Because I terminated the pregnancy, that Soul that had been hanging around us waiting to enter the family was able to get done with us what was necessary, without having to manifest through me in a physical body. Instead, it was able to do it in a few short visits with both my husband and myself, leaving us free from the added effort of raising another child and leaving itself free to move on to the next life into another family, also necessary for that particular entity. The last time either of us experienced that Soul it was a subtle connection that was filled on all our parts with love and gratitude.

Everyone has to live with her own actions, the women who choose to have abortions and those who choose not to. But no one is righter than the other. The "rightness" is in the set of circumstances, and no one can judge another for her choice. I thought about the experience I had had with my other pregnancies and I understand how many people can think the fetus is a human being. In my three pregnancies I was aware of the presence of the coming baby and I patted it and talked soothingly to it. My love grew as my belly grew—each time. I always thought the "baby" was in me, growing, getting itself ready to be born. But now I know that actually what I was talking to was outside of my body. Near me but outside and staying close. What I was talking to was Soul, that was "hanging out" with me and the rest of us in the family to see if this was where it belonged in the coming life.

What was inside my body was only the home of a human being, being built. A little body making ready to come out and house Soul. If the Soul checking me out decided this was not a good environment, it would leave for a different little baby body in another woman, a preferable future, and another Soul would take its place. If something was physically wrong with the fetus another Soul might not be willing to come in unless it decided to burn off some Karma in that particular way. If no Soul chose to enter, the baby body would die.

This business of Soul being outside the body till birth might be explained by the experience many of us have had while at a funeral or wake and feeling the presence of the person who had just died. Someone we may have known well or loved, and yet we knew this presence or energy of this person was not coming from the body in the casket but more like filling the space around the event, the funeral or wake. It is much the same thing.

So you see that our relationship does exist with our yet unborn baby, but it has little to do with the biological matter within us. The body is only a rented home for Soul and so abortion is not the sin we fear it to be.

# Song Of Myself

There is that in me—I do not know what it
  is—
    but I know it is in me.

Wrench'd and sweaty—calm and cool then
  my body
    becomes
I sleep—I sleep long.
I do not know it—it is without name—it is a
  word unsaid;
It is not in any dictionary, utterance,
  symbol.

Something it swings on more than the earth
  I swing on;
to it the creation is the friend whose
    embracing awakes me.

Perhaps I might tell more. Outlines! I plead
  for my
    brothers and sisters.

Do you see, O my brothers and sisters?
It is not chaos or death—it is form, union,
  plan—it
    is eternal life—it is Happiness.

Walt Whitman
*Leaves of Grass* (Arranged in Verse)

## chapter four

# THE DAILY BUSINESS
## Choosing and Working

My mom was shocked when she came to Boston to visit me shortly after my father's death. She wasn't strong on her own legs yet and her identity which had been buried along with her husband had yet to be reborn. She came to visit me in the apartment I shared with my roommate, Barbara. One of the expectations all along was to have me find a nice brainy Ivy Leaguer from Harvard, or at the very least, M.I.T. She was appalled to meet the man I was in love with down at his place—a rather charming old brownstone, with a yard full of cats in Roxbury. Ron had greeted us friendly enough with his intense teal-blue eyes and bright red beard. This was the year 1957. He also smelled mildly of turpentine and resembled pictures of Jesus Christ. I had recently abandoned the relationship I had been having with my "Student of Promise" that everyone was excited about. He was nice enough, to be fair, and even though the chemistry was lacking, the thing that scared me the most was that I could clearly see my destiny wrapped up in his goals. Of course, all of this was instinct. I had no clarity on the matter. As soon as I let go of the basic "good marriage plan," I found myself reeling in love with my blue-eyed Van Gogh. Of course, he was all too cool and detached to admit any feeling on his part for me, but we had planned to run away to New York together to where the "real painting" was happening, much to the dismay of our Boston teachers.

My mother's visit left me guilt-ridden and devastated. As my little sister pointed out, the timing was poor and I was killing mother. Angry and depressed, I broke the relationship off and with it went my courage. I was left in a trap facing my loneliness and the promise of mediocrity. I guess I saw Ron at the time as a ticket to my "self." After a few nights of drenching the pillow, I knew I could do it on my own. If running to New York where "Art was happening" was good enough for us, then surely it would be good for me.

I had only been to New York once before, with my father for one of my adolescent birthdays. It was Christmas time and I was overwhelmed by the holiday bustle, Schwartz's window and the Stage Delicatessen. Despite the persistence of my Uncle George sending clippings from the *Daily News* and the *Daily Mirror* showing mangled bodies of young girls on New York streets, I went. Scared as my mother, I went anyway.

I found a little room overlooking the river. Delighted, I promptly set up shop, began painting and faced some very lonely and broke days. This decision to go to New York was one of the two most important decisions of my life. It was then that I proved to myself that I had found a way out of the expectation created years ago for me. It wasn't that I was running from anything really, but rather toward my own unknown potential which would have been hidden from me had I remained among the familiar. So here I was, holed up in a room on the windy corner of Riverside Drive and 141st, a block from the heart of Spanish Harlem. I was alone and poor and ecstatic.

As I got to know the city a little, I found a part-time job in Sterns Department Store and moved downtown to where the artists were. First, I had an apartment for forty-two dollars a month, high upon the sixth floor above a Chinese laundry and an Italian shoemaker. I have already mentioned my stair syndrome, so this was just another challenge. This challenging was really getting to be fun. The avenues on either side of me had many languages, costumes and aromas. On

First Avenue, I could buy just two fresh eggs for breakfast and one roll or a loaf of black bread. I could choose from magnificent Ukranian Easter eggs, elaborately embroidered white, sheer peasant blouses and wool, woven floral babushkas of enormous size. Of course, all I could afford were the eggs and bread and fruit and a bottle of Chilean wine as there was no money for anything but food and rent. Upstairs, I had furniture which I found on the street—a heavily enameled blue table and two red chairs, a mattress on the floor in one room and a black metal stool in the third room which also contained paint, paper, canvas and easel. It was out of the window of that room that a fire escape grew, and where I grew a red geranium. Never again was I able to grow such a happy geranium as out that window on Seventh Street. That geranium and I were close friends as I used to spend many hours on the fire escape drinking coffee and watching laundry, so carefully arranged on the crisscross lines between all the brick buildings. I was learning to love my own company.

Later, when I had my loft on Maiden Lane, I had this immense superiority over women who had gotten married to artists and dropped their own art to have babies. I am now horrified at what a snob I'd been, thinking they had sold out. At that time there was no sisterhood and woman artists were highly competitive with each other as well as women in general. There just wasn't room for all of us at the top. My only interest was making good paintings and getting approval from my colleagues who were for the most part men. The paintings that had an influence on me were all done by men. Franz Kline excited me most with his powerful black and white giants. It's no wonder that I was into making big, gutsy canvases. Hanging out at the Cedar Bar, embroiled in smokey conversations at interconnecting booths, the passion, the intellectualism, and the building of late night loft parties.

By now, months later, Ron and I were seeing a lot of each other, but it wasn't sweet between us. I swung off to work at a New Hampshire hotel for the summer in order to get out of the heat and clarify my heart, which I promptly lost to a young trumpet player with the hotel band. He was tall and beautiful and played a mean horn. But I stayed true to Ron, much to the dismay of my sweet musician, the rest of the band and myself. September came and I landed back in New York, only to find the place had been violently robbed. Ron and I were reunited, this time it was Potrero Hill in San Francisco. It was a magnificent place to be and we felt better about each other. We found a houseboat on the bay surrounded by wild roses and rosemary bushes. Seals could be seen out the front door, playing. At high tide, water shloshed up under the houseboat which was resting on stilts. At low tide, it was "Mud Flat." We repaired the broken windows, painted out the obscenities and set up two studios. The big room held a double bed, a wood cook stove, a table and some chairs and the only sink I ever had that came to the proper height. Jazz, poetry, Chinese food, Mexican sweaters and leather sandals. We lived off the meager sale of paintings. In California nobody wore black as in New York, and the sun shone a lot of the time. But we began to miss the East.

Back in New York, a friend recommended we take a look at Hoboken across the river. We laughed. Then two other friends recommended the same thing, so we stopped laughing. We grabbed a ferry to the other side and checked it out. Large, cheap and only twelve minutes to Times Square. We found a store front at 306 River Street and settled in, married and pregnant.

I loved the secret of having a baby growing inside of me, but suddenly, who was I as a painter? Here I was enjoying my womanbody in a brand new way and not knowing how to paint "like a woman." My identity had become a pot of cabbage soup. I started looking at Grace Hartigan and Joan Mitchell and they didn't do it for me. Now they do, but then they didn't. Maybe I was threatened. I tried to paint flowers and felt like a fool. No substance, no guts—not the way I was painting them. Ron was building a bookstore in the Carnegie Hall building and had brought home a stack of black and white picture postcards showing the building. The postcards were interesting in themselves, but I began covering them with collage. There were so many to play with, I could take all the chances I wanted. The best part was keeping an eye on the gutter for found objects.

Forgetting about the self-conciousness of strong work, weak work, I became lost in the stacks of exquisite tiny collages. The piles got higher and the work came easier, but more and more beautiful. I stopped. Because it was too easy, I stopped. I thought, to be valid, a struggle had to take place and so I threw a gift away.

After three years in Hoboken, and the joyous birth of Adam, we spent a year again in sunny Southern California and then back to New York. This time, we landed in a three-room apartment on Fifth Street and by April 10th, we had a constantly crying Jennifer Day. The IUD the hospital gave me went astray and by the following April we had a fortunately mellow Elizabeth Anne. I was beginning to learn about those ex-painter housewives I had so easily condemned.

Within the past year Judy Chicago had come to town. I had a conflict in schedule so I missed seeing her.

A week ago standing before my sister's shelves of books I noticed *Through the Flower* by Judy Chicago which I promptly became absorbed in. Here was a woman who had suffered the same private struggle as myself, the same isolation I experienced as a woman in the arts without other women. The first person that understood that invisibility and confusion of being.

Through reading Chicago this past week many things became clear. Things about my art and my anger at the time I was painting. I was well aware of the isolation and my lack of understanding of it. I knew I was different. Different from the men and different from the women. In those smoky booths were the men, my theoretical colleagues and the women that they "liked." As far as I recall, aside from the "stars" there was only one other serious woman painter among the individuals that hung out in the Cedar Bar, and for some reason we didn't connect. Often in the same smokey conversation, our eyes rarely met. Both trying to minimize the fact of our femaleness as painters, we didn't recognize ourselves as sisters. Chicago explores this phenomenon in depth, giving me understanding into my own past. There is no one thing that stands out but the book as a whole was loaded with insights. I didn't even get far enough to acknowledge and penetrate the issues she deals with as woman artist. The issue according to her, is that female art, being different from male art (as it comes from a different set of experiences) emerges into a male standard, gets misunderstood, and consequently, lost. For me these issues existed but were unclear, and having no one to talk to about them, my attention remained on the challenges of the concepts of color, texture, and design. Looking to what lay before me as great contemporary art I was selective in my response to what moved me.

Even though deKooning was considered a god in the art world, he only served to reflect an oppressively vulgar image of womanhood which confused and angered me in the face of his fame. In the late 50's feminism still lay dormant and personal clarity on the matter was a struggle.

Kline on the other hand moved me greatly because

he did in his art what I was trying to do in my life and, therefore, my art. He broke all the molds. He burst through the barriers of established thinking and created a new way to look at things; a new appreciation of movement and a definite connection with the speed and depth of the moment. This I was learning in my life and like Chicago, I too was bringing my inner struggle into my work. But part of that struggle, the woman part, was not yet awake. However, looking back I see the femaleness and the power that thrusted sensually through my numerous self portraits. "Look," they say, "I am an artist, I am a woman."

Mainly I was consumed by spatial relationships and making color work in a non-subjective way, and as I return to this state of mind I see that my passion for art was part of the process for my own growth. The difference I discovered here is that Chicago determined to cut through her culture, pursued her history as well as the general culture and history in terms of who she was as an artist. Here I learned that for me the making of art was a process, a focal point, an energy, but it was a step in a different process, a different dharma. It was part of the learning process required for me to reach my goal of Self-realization and eventually God-realization. Chicago, in her clarity as an artist handed me that piece of revelation.

So again, I see that all life is a learning process and often we do not realize the lessons in the things we do. We do them because we have to do them. I had to make art during that period of my life. I had to also exist in that state of isolation then. Although the understanding lies within each of us it often takes another to unlock that truth for us to see.

Most of us are working women whether we punch a clock, fly a plane, run the state or run the home. I have spent mornings sitting on the toilet combing my hair while the iron was heating and the kettle screaming, trying to know whether or not my kid was really too sick to go to school. Mornings, awakened by tormented electronic sounds escaping from the alarm on the other side of the door, startling me into immediate imbalance with which to begin the oncoming day. Choices between grabbing breakfast and chancing it to work with the tank on "empty" or driving easy to work with a full tank and an empty stomach. You see, it's not the food that matters—the coffee and toast—but the mindlessness with which I can stare down into that warm, china blue cup, silently gathering myself to face the day.

I've punched early morning clocks and I've worked swing shifts. I've faced seventy-five bleary-eyed students with morning messages of great import as well as the privilege of being able to weave pictures and rugs, listening to Beethoven and having to respond to no one. As a stay-at-home wife/mother, I was always "on call" to rush to the bank, to pick up a hurt child, to chauffeur a girls' soccer team or to deal with any major or minor crises that might make its appearance under our roof. A woman by the name of Niki Scott wrote a great book called *Working Woman, A Handbook*. Because she has done such a fine job I'll keep away from covering some of the same material. She describes the frantic pace that can drown the working mother; of being pulled from all directions, and the momentum that builds up to crash speeds. One of my survival techniques for times when it seems the kids are moving just as fast and getting just as cranky, is to allow ourselves to just stop. We call in sick and don't sleep late. We get up and lounge and fortify ourselves so that when we return we can do twice the task with ease. Amazing what a break can do! ...and it's your life. It's not cheating anyone if you can make up the time/work. Actually, this is a preventative measure. I am a firm believer that most sickness is only the plea of the body and the mind for a vacation, so why spend it guiltlessly in bed with a sore throat or a nervous breakdown?

Why not fill the house with the smell of pecan swirls or corn pudding? Pile the kids in the car and go out for some quiche and conversation. Spend the day giving your plants a boost, force some bulbs in the glaring sun of a winter window and watch the approach of spring as early as January, with glorious amaryllis and narcissus. Take the time to cane a chair, paint a room, fix your bike, or dance and stretch to your favorite living room music.

It's unconventional of course to call in sick when you're really not, and harder yet when you are your own boss or everyone else's, but everyone is dispensable for a day, even if it does feel immoral. Let loose; you'll get more done in the long run and you can stop plodding through your life by coming alive.

## TIP
"The most spectacularly successful women we interviewed have been creative quitters. Barbara Marshall, now president of Welcome Wagon, says that a woman who is ready for a promotion has to have the courage to move out of a comfortable slot."[1]

## A WORD FOR HOMEMAKING
To be a good homemaker takes great skill, energy, patience and compassion. Running a home is probably one of the best training programs in endurance and flexibility a person can have. It can be creative, stimulating and fulfilling. Of course there is monotony and the dirty work, but that exists in any job. At least at home it's only physical. In the business world it's psychological, lying and cheating. For women to

---

[1]Caroline Bird and David McKay, *Everything a Woman Needs to Know to Get Paid What She's Worth* (New York: 1981).

feel less because they work at home instead of out is one of the crimes of the decade. There is a delicate balance here and what needs to be made clear is that it is not what we do but rather how we do it. The challenge in homemaking can be a lot more than the challenge of emergency, stress and the way to beat fatigue. It can be built into creating an adventurous lifestyle for self and family. Can you burst into song in your office? Do an arabesque at the elevator or catch a flying poem at the conference table? Not as easily as at the kitchen sink.

There is that age-old myth that man envies woman for being the ultimate creator, the producer of human beings. The ultimate, as I see it is not the ability to produce them, but to raise them into healthy and whole young adults, and this takes all the tuning in, patience and love that it takes to be a Brancusi or a Matisse.

How much we get paid for what we do somehow has always, in the back of our minds, been a measure of the worth of our existence, and how we feel about ourselves. In our own environment among our peers, such as other homemakers, painters or poets, we feel good. We respect each other's seriousness and labor and we have a standard to meet. But in the world at large we lose that. Nobody else knows. Homemakers find themselves wondering if what they do is actually work, although they very well know it is, despite the fact that the world keeps telling them it isn't. It takes a lot of strength to keep the external world from defining our identities for us according to our earning power. The very fact that a ball player or a rock star can earn so much more than a poet or a maid is absurdly arbitrary. We all do what we must do and should know that we are doing that thing by choice, and if we are not, we had better look at that thing again and reconsider, because the situation is one that we have created somewhere down the line.

"A job as human right is a principal that applies to men as well as women. But women have more cause to fight for it. The phenomenon of the "Working Woman" has been held responsible for everything from male impotence to the rising cost of steak...(because according to one explanation, we are no longer staying home to prepare the cheaper slower-cooking cuts, as good wives should). Unless we include a job as part of every citizen's right to autonomy and personal fulfillment, women will continue to be vulnerable to someone else's idea of what 'need' is."[2]

Take the time to get a career instead of "working at a job." Find something you like to do and remember you want to work smart not hard. Trust that you can do it and just go ahead and do it. The word determination has a lot to do with endurance and keeping a steady eye on the goal. There are many "how to" books in the library to consult as well as many people in your community whose job it is to assist you. Do some research. For some serious contemplating, read "The Cinderella Complex" by Colette Dowling, published by Summit Books.

"More and more women are starting their own businesses, to find work in a tight job market, to find freer expression of their creative and management abilities, and to put into practice their own ideas of how the business world should operate. Whatever

[2]Gloria Steinem, "Why Women Work," *Ms. Magazine* (New York: March 1979), pp. 46-52, 90-92.

the motives or combination of them, the self employed woman is an idea whose time has come."[3]

I was never able to enter into any social situation with any specific identity except that I was myself. There were times when I didn't know who that self was because "it" was changing and at those times I usually avoided the kind of social situation that would have brought me down. I was myself, nevertheless, and I think that following one's nose keeps one in touch with being oneself. I have never really set up goals for myself until very recently. People say, "Well, I'll go to school and get my Masters; I'll get my PhD. and then I'll do this and then I'll do that," and they've got the whole thing pretty well lined up and that is fine and for some people it really works. For me, my life has constantly been in a state of change; transition and experience, excitement and adventure—and sure there have been moments of insecurity. But I don't believe the people we think are secure are really the secure ones, because security is not financial the way we've been programmed to think it is. Being secure within oneself is the important thing, the foundation. I have always known that I would survive, because I have listened to my little inner voice that brought me from one situation to the next, from some of the very craggy places, very scary. Some of them so scary and painful that it would be too difficult to even consider at the time I was going through it. But then, coming through it and looking back at it, they were enormous growth periods. It was a thrust into a cleaner, clearer view in terms of perception and capabilities. My whole life has been based on that and I think it all comes down to trusting yourself, doing

[3]Heidi Fiska and Karen Zehring, "How to Start Your Own Business," Ms. Magazine (New York: April 1976), p. 55.

your best and letting yourself be.

What happened for me was, as a reaction to how other people lived, I began very naively, very unconsciously to compose my life with spontaneity and color. I continued to do so knowing that each part was a part of a larger whole and that the perimeter of the page was the birth to death of one lifetime, and so there were large open spaces, and dark heavy lines, yellow and red explosions, blue and lavender expanses and constant movement, constant change. Always striving for the now, not knowing how to be in the now, but as I look back I see I was completely in the now. Only my intellectualized concept of what that meant put it outside my reality. I don't know if we can ever learn to live without constantly jumping on our own backs.

How this gets back to work is this: We, you and I, can do anything. We are the ones that form the molds for ourselves in very subtle ways. All this business about inadequacy and insecurity in women is true. If We Accept It. You can be overpowered by the media, by thought forms, by the attitude of others only if you allow it. The truth is you can do anything you want to if you really set your mind to it.

"Our pleasure is to do every day, the work of the day, to cut our hair and not want blue eyes."[4]

It took me awhile to learn about goals, and I did a lot of meandering, but that was my way. That's the form my learning process took. I covered a lot of ground, worked through a lot of karma, found a lot of love, and felt lost and unidentifiable at times. But I have managed to come in line with myself because of

[4]Linda Simon, *Biography of Alice B. Toklas* (New York: 1977), p. 256.

a distinct stubbornness which helped me to avoid being influenced by others, by titles, by experts, or by those trying to keep me down. Making a determined effort to be influenced only by my own instincts, I listened not to my mind but to my little inner voice, which when listened to, never failed me.

In the times we are living it is increasingly important that we get ourselves trained and marketable and that we begin to recognize our capabilities. In order to succeed economically and emotionally, we should not think of work as a temporary thing, a stop gap till we marry, or the kids are through school, or any number of limitations. In doing this we create a built-in and often hidden dependency. We also limit our potential if in the back of our minds we are going to be saved and taken care of by a phantom provider after a year or two or a decade or two.

For work that is satisfying both financially and emotionally, a realistic attitude about independence is important. I see this clearly in my two daughters. Both of them have witnessed financial struggle all their lives and so have become more goal oriented than I ever was and more realistic about economic independence. Yet I would not describe them as materialistic, because they are fully aware of themselves as individuals and spiritual beings. This is the kind of attunement that they are striving to maintain.

The attitude of competence and independence in combination with the recognition of our spiritual selves are the ingredients helpful in maintaining a balanced life.

I still don't make much money, but I have found what is important to me. What's important to you will be different and you'll find your own way to do it if you haven't already. Just remember that the mold you make now is what will happen for or to you in the future, either in this lifetime or another. Often we ask for something, wish for something then forget about it. Later it comes around and we don't make the connection that we alone set it up. So be sure that what you want is really what you want, and then go for it. Set the mold, let go of it, and suddenly to your amazement, there it'll be. The job, the position, whatever, down to the real essence of what it is you are after. Forever being careful not to step on all the toes in front of you, for to hurt someone else is only hurting yourself. Is anything worth it when every action has reaction in full measure?

I'm a stalwart believer in "If It's To Be It Will Be." You have to work for it but you can't hunger after it, it might bring on indigestion. Set the wheels in motion, then slip it into automatic while you find another thing to do. Nothing is so important that we need to hang on gasping for it. Look the other way, at the new bees of spring, the child in the tree, or the cat on the windowsill with misty pink cherry blossoms framing his form.

Life is about many things and when you know that, it is seen by the world and you have nothing to fear, everything to gain.

## Defeat and Victory

"No matter what happens, refuse to take it tragically. Absolutely repudiate a crown of martyrdom. If you cannot laugh at yourself (which is the best medicine of all) at least try to handle the difficulty in an objective way—as though it concerns someone else. To be tragic is to accept defeat. To refuse to be tragic is to assume victory. Know that you can be victorious if you insist upon victory."[1]

---

[1]Darwin Gross, *Gems of Soul* (California: 1980), p. 15.

chapter five

# DEALING WITH FEAR
## Protecting Our Young
## Recognizing Our Own Demons

One day while reading Gail Sheehy's book, *Passages,* it occurred to me that I hadn't even thought about terror. It's a feeling I hadn't experienced for awhile and when I began looking back, I remembered.

As a mother of young children I had a terror that they couldn't be watched closely enough, that if I wasn't paying attention, calamity was inevitable. This fortunately was not a constant frame of mind, but it did invade my consciousness from time to time. It became a deadly fantasy that went something like this: In the night when I was asleep, little adventurous and investigative Jenny would crawl out of bed, across the rooms and out onto Paradise Hill, the steep road that lay in shadows in front of our house. The thought of it forced me to drive at creeping speeds when we ourselves were out late at night. Who knows, there could be a baby at the bottom of any hill.

When we lived in Maine, our house sat at the crest of French Hill, where my 6, 7, and 9 year olds were fond of riding the "banana seat" someone had generously bequeathed to them. Terror struck as lumber trucks could be heard making their way up from the bottom of the hill, or bullet-speeding cars taking a running start to zoom up and over our blind spot. With twenty acres to play in, it was the road that intrigued them, the smooth, hard black top that stretched like a snake before our house. On occasion they would beg me to let them go down to fish at Michael Stream off the bridge at the bottom of the hill. I was terrified to let them go, not only because of the road, but the strange folks from the next town who, because of generations of inbreeding, had sometimes exhibited peculiar senses of humor. During those times, Ron compounded my misery by calling me a Jewish mother, even though all the mothers in those isolated areas shared the same dread. The vulnerability of children is so far beyond their innocent, adventuresome minds that it's a wonder we can breathe at all during these years. But what I found is that when you put your attention on something you give it energy, so the more you worry over these bizarre possibilities, the more you are likely to have them occur.

When we begin to understand about karma, the law of cause and effect, we can begin to drop so many of our anxieties. All we have to do is carry out our responsibilities with love and awareness and that's it. If, then, something happens we do not have to blame ourselves, for the experience is for that individual, whether it is our child or our neighbor. Often what appears to be a negative experience is neither negative nor positive. It simply is. Each experience, whether it appears to be negative or positive, is for the benefit of the experiencer. Not in an obvious way necessarily, but in terms of the big picture; the totality of our many lives, it is to our advantage—another step toward perfection. As an example, we could possibly finally be paying off a large karmic debt we no longer need hanging over our heads. I find it rather sad sometimes when someone is outraged because of how an individual treated them or, to bring it into a broader sense, the prejudice of one group toward another. The people in the oppressive group will one day have to return as the oppressed, and so it goes. Thusly, we can look backward at the oppressed of the world and rightly assume that they at one time had been the oppressors. I am not speaking here of religions or races but of the individuals who chose to incarnate into the religion or race. If we are in the

-64-

position of living comfortably and happily but have respect for all living things, we have no doubt earned the right; if we are ripping off then we are not having respect for all living things and therefore will become the ripped off in a future time. There is no sin in affluence. There is no sin, period. There is only karma and in the long run, justice for all.

"Sometimes you'll find that through a negative experience that you have gained a realization that nothing else in this world could have done for you."[2]

Terror is a state none of us enjoy, but it, too, has its own place in the educational process of growth.

After reading *The Bell Jar* by Sylvia Plath one time, I became so absorbed in her psyche that when I was done I had taken on her identity. I stood in a sundrenched winter living room in a house that was empty that day. I stood there before a stove pipe, leaning against the warmth of the stove, staring into the flap of the damper flopping back and forth. I was strange. Scared to the point that if I took my eyes off the damper I would have immediately gone insane. It was as if that black thing, silently opening and closing, was a mandala designed specifically to keep Marge Curtis alive that day. I hung on to it with every breath, refusing to blink. It was my only lifeline. I couldn't move or blink or think. I thought it was me that it was the end of. I didn't know that upon reading that book I had opened myself up to the consciousness of Sylvia Plath, not knowing how to be Sylvia Plath. For three days I had walked around feeling like

---

[2]Darwin Gross, *Gems of Soul* (California: 1980), p. 115.

someone else, but I didn't think much about it. I just kept being busy, not tuning in, and I was finally captured in my own house with my own utter terror. Frozen in time, I stood unmoving, my mind a fragment.

A voice inside kept telling me to go lie down on the couch. I knew it was death and tried not to listen. The little voice kept telling me to walk over to the couch and lie down. In the winter sunlight of my own living room, I was an alien. I could ignore it no longer, death was beckoning. I took a deep breath and made ready. Slowly moving my eyes away from the mandala, I walked toward the couch with all the power I could muster. I lay down as if for sacrifice. My poor family; what would they think when they found me? Slowly I lifted my legs onto the couch and lay back with my eyes closed, ready for the end. To my amazement I was suddenly overcome by the peaceful presence of myself. After three days I had returned. I had let go and my little voice had once again been able to take care of me, making my relationship with It ever stronger.

I had been thinking how strange it was that I had forgotten about terror and the importance of sharing mine with you. Terror is something I have not experienced since I have become aware that death is indeed not what it seems. That all we do is leave our bodies behind, just as we do in the dream state. All of our negative traits are based upon fear, and all of our fear is based upon two things, attachment and death. Attachment being the dependency on people or things, and death being an illusion. What a trick for the negative forces to play on humanity, to keep us blinded from our own immortality. I, for one, am no longer bound by this trick. I know I am Soul and that Soul exists because of God's love for it and that Soul is eternal. Knowing this, how can we choose fear over freedom?

# Bali Hai Calls Mama

As I was putting away the groceries
I'd spent the morning buying
for the week's meals I'd planned
around things the baby could eat,
things my husband would eat
and things I should eat
because they aren't too fattening,
late on a Saturday afternoon
after flinging my coat on a chair
and wiping the baby's nose
while asking my husband
what he'd fed it for lunch
and whether
the medicine I'd bought for him
had made his cough improve,
wiping the baby's nose again,
checking its diaper,
stepping over the baby
who was reeling to and from
the bottom kitchen drawer
with pots, pans and plastic cups,
occasionally clutching the hem of my skirt
and whining to be held;
I was half listening to the football game
from the next room
and waiting for the phone
which never rings for me
to ring for me
and someone's voice to say
I could forget about handing back
my students' exams which I'd had for a
    week,
that I was right about The Wasteland,
that I'd been given a raise,
all the time wondering
how my sister was doing

whatever happened to my old lover(s)
and why my husband wanted
a certain brand of toilet paper;
and I wished I hadn't, but I'd bought
another fashion magazine that promised
to make me beautiful by Christmas,
and there wasn't room for the creamed corn
and every time I opened the door
the baby rushed to grab whatever was on the
   bottom shelf
of the refrigerator which meant I constantly
   had to wrestle
jars of its yucky food out of its sticky hands
and I stepped on the baby's hand and the
   baby was screaming
and I dropped the bag of cake flour I'd
   bought to make cookies with
and my husband rushed in to find out what
   was wrong because the baby
was drowning out the sound of the
   touchdown although I had scooped
it up and was holding it in my arms so its
   crying was inside
my head like an echo in a barrel and I was
   running cold water
on its hand while somewhere in the back of
   my mind wondering what
to say about The Wasteland and whether I
   could get away with putting
broccoli in a meatloaf when

suddenly through the window
came the wild cry of geese.[3]

---

[3]Marilyn Nelson Waniek.

chapter six

# BOOGIE ON THROUGH
## Step by Step

In the beginning, as artists, it had been fine to denounce materialism and strive for higher ideals as a creator of depth and beauty, but as the years continued I found myself suddenly engulfed by hungry children and the self-made trap of involuntary poverty. Living poor for the longest time certainly had its frustrations, having to sometimes choose between soup and cereal, but in a way it was satisfying, because it showed me how much I could do without. And if I ever got sick of it, I could always pick up and leave. After all, I was a middle class girl with a college education and this was only a statement I was making in the process of rearranging values. Somewhere in the back of my mind I thought if it didn't work, I could get out. I was dead wrong. I, like all the ghetto mothers, had to struggle with the decision of which to bring upstairs first, the kids and the groceries, or the kids and the carriage or the groceries and the carriage. Which was most likely to get stolen off the street, and where were the kids safest alone? Downstairs under the lazy eye of the neighbor or up in the apartment? And don't forget, I was not one to run very fast up stairs.

The few friends I had were unmarried couples, making paintings, going to openings, bars and poetry readings, but I could never pay for the babysitter. My old friends didn't have time to come by in the afternoons when I needed them. Sometimes they'd stop by after dinner with a bottle of wine and relate to Ron and I as a couple, like them. But, that's not what I was. I was a young mother in isolation, needing someone to speak with on my own terms.

When it was just Adam and we lived in Hoboken, it was easier. One "good" baby was a snap and we lived on the ground floor. My friends at that time were three mad, genius, homosexual men. They enjoyed the whole notion of the creation of a human being and the progress we both made. They were involved in the art scene, were supportive and funny and made the best coq au vin I ever tasted.

But in New York, after the birth of new baby Jenn, New York Clinic slipped an IUD mistakenly through my uterus into my abdominal wall, bringing within the year, beautiful new baby Liz and major abdominal surgery. Now I wasn't playing house anymore. This was for real. Living in the three bedroom apartment and later the loft, I had little opportunity for a social life or for meeting mothers in the same glorious dilemma as myself. I say glorious because in a way it was glorious, if indeed it was lonely and hard. There was the joy of growing intimacy and the beautiful beginnings of each child. The first step, the first word, the contented and blissful way each tiny head would drop back, satiated from sucking their fill of milk. There were joys no one in my world understood.

In Tomkins Square Park, where I used to take the children, there were very proud, very young Ukranian mothers who wheeled their babies through the park in those beautiful deep blue highrise English carriages with impeccable pink or blue satin coverlets pinned to the sides with silver clips. Sometimes they were accompanied by a mother or an aunt, but they never sat to talk, and their children never got dirty. There were some women that came singly or with a friend, pushing canvas carriages or strollers fitted with faded flannel or handknit wool blankets. They would come for an afternoon of talking and catching the sun, rocking the carriage constantly while keeping a watchful eye on the corduroy child playing in the sandbox. We shared recipes and remedies.

Most of us were married to artists and musicians. Most of us were struggling with top floor walkups, irregular incomes and men with big dreams who were home doing their "art," hustling gigs and galleries. I loved the camaraderie we shared those afternoons. There was a definite sisterhood, not that we ever called each other on the phone or went to the same parties or even knew each other's last names, but we were the same in our dedication to our children and our tolerance for our men.

We were the same in the business of our lives. We were relaxed out there on the benches where we could be ourselves. We didn't have to worry about keeping the kids quiet for our sensitive husbands or rushing to keep the beans from burning while changing a diaper. It was indeed a proud sharing until it seemed like overnight there came a change. The black women turned to ice. They suddenly sat all on one side with their backs toward us with never an explanation. That was in 1964. Since there were so many more of them than us, I often was the only white mother, and suddenly Adam, too, was left without a friend.

I stopped going to the park except to walk through on the way to Washington Square, which was across town in the Village. These excursions were saved for perfect weather days and when I got there, there were always people I knew and folk to talk to. Coming home, I'd pick up a fresh fish or a braided bread and tuck it into the carriage somewhere. But most of the time I'd cross over to the projects where there were many brand new brick buildings and a playground made of railroad tie towers and cobblestone tunnels and many other wonderful climbing toys. Here, too, I sat alone rocking the carriage with one hand and a book in the other while Lizzie softly slept inside. Jenny with her bright rosy cheeks, played by my feet, while Adam braved the high slides and scaled the wooden beams. The women here were bitter. They resented my even being there. We lived across the street in the old buildings.

In bad weather, it was me and the three kids. Ron was out on carpentry jobs a lot by then and I often wondered while gazing out at the fire escape how I'd ever make it down with just two arms and two legs if I had to. Ron was still painting as well as doing carpentry. We had no money and very few conveniences in the loft. The laundry was insurmountable. It was during those years that a great deal of distance began to creep between us. I could have hated him, but it would have gotten in my way. The parties we did go to were mostly those of people he knew or old friends of us both, very single and very free. He began to envy them, their lack of responsibilities. I began to resent them, their lack of interest and understanding. I was thoroughly involved in pre-school and baby issues by now. My kids were my life and I was going to do it right. I had become dull. There were always many attractive women available at these events, drinking and flirting, and Ron was indeed enchanting. There were pale and skinny girls with long hair and dull minds who had learned well the art of flattery. There were fashionable willowy rich girls who would come downtown to mingle with the bohemians and snag a little romance.

But I had Hannah. Hannah lived two avenues over and often we would meet and take the kids somewhere. They got along. She was married to a poet who also drove a cab, so they had a steady income and were able to have a few nice things. She even had a car on occasion so we'd go to the zoo or take a ferry to Staten Island, lugging oranges and crackers and baby bottles and it would be a regular outing. Sometimes, if we had a couple of dollars left over from grocery shopping, we'd check out the thrift stores. There were lots of good ones on the lower east side, and for two dollars you could find something really beautiful.

Hannah was in analysis. I couldn't understand it, though it was just becoming acceptable. She was pretty, and loving and strong, but very serious and especially serious about getting me to go too. It was threatening. To me it looked like she had created one healthy dependency on this man. It also looked like she was in love with him; a conversation about the most banal thing could not go by without a veritable quote from him. Hannah was honest and loving, but full of guilt, and even out of our mutual desperation, our friendship began to dissipate. ·

As I write about these days, my memory crams with images of New York in the fall. That's when I liked it best. Racing home under the darkening sky, the carriage bouncing up and down curbs, two sleeping babies, brown bundles stuffed in the basket and pulling Adam's reluctant hand while his head incessantly turned in curiosity over something. Sometimes I kept Lizzie bundled inside my thick, black coat against by body keeping us both snug. I was silently proud that all this life came out of my young body. Of course I was common among the hundreds racing home to shelter, wondering why so few could share my pride. Being needed kept me on my toes and balanced out the obstacles.

I had decided two things. One, that I had to start looking good, real good. There were too many people out there who did. The other was that since I usually couldn't get to a lot of the big artsy parties, Ron and I would try having one. It led to others. The loft was perfect. We could have two hundred people easily. Two hundred swinging, dancing, smoking people having a great time and no financial outlay. It was astounding. People came in all ages, shapes, sizes and colors. Some were famous, most were not; artists, collectors, designers, actors, poets and musicians. Some

were scruffy off the street and some were from up-
town, wearing diamonds and furs, some carrying
babies. Put to sleep near mine, nothing bothered
them. It was before the real impact of marijuana and
Viet Nam, yet both were well in existence. I had
learned how to look good. I had found a few things in
the thrift stores and some flashy remnants in the
fabric stores. I had discovered Maybelline eyeliner
and had learned how to fix my hair. I did this mostly
to attract the attention of Ron by attracting the
attention of others. I got the others, but Ron never
noticed. He was busy attracting his own attention.
But when it was over, we both collapsed on the couch
with a definite sense of well being, our wounds having
been licked, our egos having been pampered.

The following year we moved out of the city. For
some reason I was a little reluctant to go. I guess the
old fear of the "bourgeois monster" raising its boring
head was a little frightening, but ready for something
new, we took the chance. Someone had offered us a
real house for the price of the water bill and taxes in a
sheltered, shrub-filled town in New Jersey. The house
itself was dark and the yard was overgrown.
Everything out back that could be seen from a large
picture window in the kitchen was tall, bent, dry and
yellow. There were three golden willows that could be
seen down the path that connected to the back of the
Roosevelt School yard. It was a fairyland. A small
bedroom town. Most of the income was from New
York City except for the artists, and there were quite a
few of them to balance things out. Lots of mommies
with babies and pre-schoolers, people who had
interests of their own, but who were now consumed
with homemaking, bringing up kids right and
sharpening their own identities. It was then I learned
to weave, from the library books brought by the
bookmobile. Winter naptime was my time, and I
remember how I would waste most of it frantically

trying to decide how to spend the precious three quarters of an hour. Weaving, reading, exercising, having a lingering cup of coffee or hanging out the clothes while scanning for a passing deer. There was just so little time my mind raced, but I usually sat at the loom and worked out tapestries. We spent lazy afternoons around summertime pools and went to all the children's birthday parties. The kids got older. Coffee klatching turned into consciousness raising.

Now, for me, this is like another woman's story. If I knew then what I know now, things would have been a lot easier, but that was an experience I needed to go through; to become strong, to become compassionate and to learn something about the fertile poor.

In the days of young children, there is so little time to complete a thought, to mentally get from one point to another and it feels as if one never will. What happens though is that it is actually a very short time period. A flash in the pan. By the time the youngest child is in school, things can begin to change if you let them. The kids can begin to understand, listen and care if they have the foundation of love and caring, no matter how self-centered they may seem. For them, being self-centered is natural, particularly as they get older. Being self-centered is the nature of the young. Annoying as it is to us sometimes, it is their way of becoming themselves so they can survive as whole beings. If we can be the observer and watch ourselves grow along with our kids, and, although it can sometimes be very frustrating, the big thing to remember is that it is only a temporary situation and it is more our attitude that determines success or failure in our lives than the events.

We are not old and unattractive at thirty-eight as the media is so fond of telling us. Living where we are in the moment-by-moment gives us strength, and with strength comes beauty. We always fear our best years are eaten away by our children and the resentment we have for our husbands. But as I look back at all the struggle and frustration, the love and the pride wrapped up in the process of nourishing, because of the intensity and consummation of it all, the time sped by, never to be retrieved for alteration.

Taking a look now, having survived that point, I'm more myself than ever, healthier, clearer and rolling. This is not to say I didn't have many uncomfortable transitions along the way, or that there are not more in store for me, but these times are probably the greatest growth times of all. One of the best things is that now I have these people whom I nurtured into human beings, who have become my friends. Individuals themselves, sparkling, funny, near adults who are also nourishers, Adam as well as Jenn and Liz. They're there for me in my scattered moments of need, although I expect they won't always be. The in-between times, they're wrapped up in their own universes; relationships, school, jobs, direction and the process of finding their own identities.

A drive to school
a busy question
and a lot to do
I ran about and forgot to smile
but didn't notice
a song, a dance
a second chance
wait a minute
a pulse of energy
I turned to see
a desert sky
and a far reply
but I could hear it
and learned to listen
You are the warrior
and this is your adventure

The light turned green,
and I had to smile.[1]

I could have remained angry, remembered the wounds that were never understood and carried our differences to this day, but somehow, unconsciously I carried the sameness instead, and was able to begin to see the isolation, fears and struggles of Ron's life, the flip side. Two people, sleeping in the same bed for 20 years. Some of those years we were enemies. For me, he was an intruder. He wanted sex when I was the most exhausted from a day of frustration, household chores and keeping peace among children, parents and bill collectors. He, feeling frightened of not being able to provide, bearing the responsibility and the guilt feeling, shut out from our established intimacy, just wanting a little contact. And even if some of it was to relieve tension, or to get to sleep, so what? Some of it was for warmth and comfort, some for communication. Being tired in our own worlds, we didn't care to satisfy each other's needs, so often the escape turned inward into bitterness or outward into anger or the need for other people. But from time to time we laughed, talked and shared what we could, the honesty we knew, the truth as we understood it. It kept us delicately connected, and with some compassion and respect if not real companionship. But that was only some of those years and I think the effort we made to remain in touch through those hardest years allowed us to eventually recognize that the dilemma was not a contest of Ron vs. Marge nor Male vs. Female, but the dilemma of Life. So instead of fighting to win battle after battle, we finally discovered that if we could join together we could win the war. The war of the way things are, and as

------

[1] Adam Be Curtis.

partners we slowly learned to laugh at ourselves as well as each other, give each other space and have compassion in the situations we didn't understand, trusting the other within our own reality. This is a marriage born of naivety, reared in resentment and finally, realizing not only love, but fun in the presence of each other's company while remaining two very distinct individuals.

I like to think, since I realize upon looking back, that I was no bargain either, I had plenty to learn, so what we did in actuality was we each married potential.

The male/female dilemma will never change. Oh, hopefully, we'll have ERA, reproductive freedom, and supportive and encouraging beginnings the way our brothers have as children, but the dilemma of the distinction between male and female will never really disappear. With people communicating better than ever before and with men becoming more aware of our needs, and with us, now that so many of us are in the job market, understanding the pressures they've had to deal with all along, we are becoming more aware of their needs. Things are better than they were and hopefully, will continue to improve with a lot of effort on everyone's part. But there will always be problems, as everything is relative. So in the long run, it comes down to attitude, our own personal attitude. When our attitude begins to change, allowing us to see beyond our own discomforts and restrictions, then our lives will follow, becoming creative, challenging and satisfying existences. It is possible that those of us that have the hardest times as women, probably doled out the hardest times as men in other incarnations. It is a cop-out to think of ourselves as victims. We are only victims according to the situation we created for ourselves, either in this lifetime or another. That is the Law of Karma, the Law of Cause and Effect.

Our suffering is twofold. It is there to teach us something we need to learn and it is there to give us the opportunity to pay off our accumulated debts. It is there to give us the chance to turn naivete into wisdom.

These lower planes—physical, astral (emotional), causal (memory), mental and etheric (intuition) are designed to give us the runaround, to drive us finally through despair or some sudden golden moment of light into the awareness of the big picture. Each one of us individually must come to the realization that the situation lies within and not without. When one societal problem is solved another will rise to take its place. There have always been the dominant and the recessive, the active and the passive. There has always been war and injustice and there always will be. Peace does not and will not exist on earth. Ever. This is why it is up to us to recognize that the real changes to be made are those within, that we are really responsible for ourselves and every situation we find ourselves in. Once that begins to happen, we begin to see that we are no longer bound by the reality of our physical surroundings. We as individuals are capable of lifting ourselves out of our human state of consciousness into a spiritual state where there is all the peace, love, and joy we have always been looking for. Then, we can bring this experience, this knowingness that has no sexual limitation, down into our daily lives. We may continue to have the same problems, but by having a greater perspective we see how tiny the problems really are within the totality of our own big picture, and that nothing bothers us half as much anymore. It is at that point that we begin to be effective in this world, that we begin to not only "give love" but "be loved" without expectations of any kind. This is truth, and it works. Each and every one of us has the capability to perceive it if we have the guts. If we can let go of our limited reality and open up to a far greater one in order to prove to ourselves what truth really is. We will each some day do this. Either in this lifetime or a hundred lifetimes from now. The warriors will do it now.

All night long I looked through
the dictionary but could not
find the words.

Reps, *Gold Fish Signatures*
(Vermont 1962)

When do we space out? Usually when
we're alone feeling free or in a situation we
don't like. Remember the window as seen
from your desk at school? Where did you
go? And as a mother person, folding diapers,
sweeping floors........

Kids go play in the back
I'm cleaning here
dreaming here.

Broken blossoms like
lace drift between
my work and me.

chapter seven

# SPACE OUT WITHOUT GUILT
## The Planes of Existence

God, having no genitals, is neither male nor female. Not being in style today, IT exists anyway and is not subject to the taste of the times. Trying to squeeze ITs totality into any one religion would be something like trying to squeeze our universe through a funnel into a mason jar. God is all and therefore, in all, religion or not. Truth IS God, the force, the source whatever word you like and "IT" can be found everywhere. The understanding of Truth and the acceptance of and love of "IT" is limited only by our own state of consciousness, how far are we willing to open our hearts and how much risk we are willing to take. Reality is only an agreement among people that something exists, but different cultures have different realities, and how do we measure to find out whose reality is the most real? What about the visions of the saints in ancient times? Today, when we have a vision or a mystical experience, a sudden glimpse or recognition into another reality, we dare not tell anyone. There are many who have broken through the prison of limitation through the use of psychedelic drugs to discover a far greater consciousness within themselves. There are many who have stumbled into that vastness on their own in the dream state or the twilight zone we're all familiar with.

For me, the first indication that there was anything beyond my view happened one night within a year after my father died. I was stretched out on my dormitory bed, relaxing after class and waiting to go down to dinner. I was in a very relaxed state and started falling into a semi-doze when suddenly I was transported through starry galaxies at great speeds until I found myself quite still in the presence of my father. It was a most surprising and ecstatic reunion, and yet it puzzled me greatly, for I could not see or hear him, smell or feel him and yet we were in intimate juxtaposition. I was flabbergasted that none of my senses were working and still I knew him, the essence of him, more him than the man who gave me bear hugs as a little girl or the one who terrorized me at Sunday morning brunches as I was growing up fat. He was there. I was there. Above time and space we lingered in Soul body. I gently slid back into my body and with eyes wide open in disbelief and joy I tried to return to that place of bliss and comfort, but I was stuck, as if it had never happened. It wasn't just that I had found my father, but that I had found out about death. I didn't eat much that night and I kept my secret to myself for years—all the while searching in libraries for information on such phenomenon.

There was some information available, and soon I began finding people who had also experienced such things. The adventure, the mystery, it was only beginning. That first awareness of out of body travel was an experience given to me "by the higher ups" to shake me loose from my previous restrictive beliefs. But, as I said, that was only the beginning. There were many steps along the way and many dangers to survive. In my search I latched onto individuals I'd come across who looked to me as if they "knew" something I wanted to know. As in the case of Dr. Richard Alpert (Ram Dass). His search for the truth was a result of his experience and change of values through LSD. However, there was similarity in that both Alpert and myself, among millions of other isolated individuals, had stumbled onto a path in search of looking for someone who "knew," so that we too could "find out." We, by the millions, as individuals are always in this process. Some consciously and some unconsciously. Most people are content to stay where they are, in the familiar where they have mastered the rules and the skills of survival for their state of being and their environment. But this experience was only my "conscious" beginning of the conscious search, as was the psychedelic experience the launching pad for Alpert's search. Mine had started long before I was aware that I was searching.

Alan Watts, in his book, *Does It Matter?*, has an entire essay called psychedelics and the religious experience. I personally feel that the drug experience is a dangerous way of beginning a spiritual journey because it can easily become a trap and there is so much illusion involved. I think it's worth reading although it's not my way to go.

I was intrigued at one time by the sorcery and knowledge of the Carlos Castaneda books. When Don Juan's student asks him why drugs, Don Juan answers, because you are dumb. He points out how a person so closed minded and locked into reason needs something external like the "magic mushroom" to crack open the consciousness. Don Juan's books became one of the glimmers of hope in my search, and the suffering and joy were phenomenal, but still, for me there were questions unanswered. These few things I have mentioned, as extraordinary as they are, can only bring us to very limited states. If we use any of this carefully as a stepping stone, calling on God or whatever Spiritual Force we are in touch with to assist us in our spiritual journey, we may not get stuck in the illusion of our own power. Here, too, is where we must understand about Karma; we reap what we sow, what goes round, comes round, there's no free lunch, there is always a cashier around the corner. This is what comes from the desire of power for oneself rather than the good of the whole. When we begin to see this we may even begin to see that we of ourselves are powerless, without the presence of Spirit. Here are some of my findings through my personal experience found through the teachings of Eckankar.

There are the five planes. 1. The *physical* being at the bottom, which is often referred to as the ashcan of the universe. What some people think of as hell is really right here. There is nothing lower to sink to except in our own consciousness. 2. Slightly above that is the *astral* plane, the same place which is also referred to as the emotional plane. It is where astral projection, death and drugs usually bring us. 3. Then there is the *causal* plane or world which is the seed plane, holding all memory or the seeds of existence. 4. Then there is the *mental* plane which is self-explanatory, with the etheric being the higher part of the mental realm. These four worlds are the total reality of most beings in civilization. They are the worlds of duality. They are composed of the positive and negative forces, the yin and the yang, the masculine and the feminine and all the opposites; the worlds of duality. They are ruled by the negative forces, which is why there are so many problems; personal, environmental, societal, etc. Each one of us has a body to correspond to these planes. The physical body holds the same vibration as the physical plane, the astral body or the emotional body is what many people use when they are on drugs. It brings them to the same vibrational rate as the astral plane. This plane, like our world, is very beautiful in places and very horrible in places. It has a population of good guys and bad guys and all the in-betweens, much like here, but it is a slightly finer vibration and is a little speeded up. It is also the place where many reside after death until their next incarnation. It is the body we use in our emotional states, the tingling we get or the internal shaking we get in extreme emotion—love, hate, anger, fear. When many people talk about leaving their body through the use of mushrooms, meditation, trance, astral projection, etc., it is their physical body they leave behind. This is as far as they go. Not all people, but most. The causal body contains the memory of our past lives and we drop the astral and physical bodies to visit the causal plane and to travel the time track, past, present and future. It all exists simultaneously and is available to us on this plane with the use of this body.

Beyond that is the mental body. It is the mind body and has the same vibrational rate as the mental plane—higher than those planes below. This is an area where most of the world's religions exist. It is indeed a heavenly realm and the area to which many great masters like Jesus, Buddha, etc. have tried to lead their people. To travel to this realm, one must drop the physical, astral and causal bodies to experience this highest point of the worlds of duality. The etheric plane is the higher part of the mental realm and the last step before the void. Jung, in speaking of these lower worlds as "real life," says:

> "...day and night, birth and death, happiness and misery, good and evil. We are not even sure that one will prevail against the other, that good will overcome evil, or joy defeat pain. Life is a battleground. It always has been, and always will be; and if it were not so, existence would come to an end."[1]

However, there is more. There is the void. That area the eastern teachings promise us with enlightenment. It is a vast area of darkness which one cannot get through without the guidance and protection of a Spiritual Traveler or ECK Master; one who comes and goes through the void to the other side often enough to be able, if we choose, to show us the way.

---

[1]Carl G. Jung, *Man and His Symbols* (New York: 1964), pp 87-88.

A WORD OF WARNING: Do not attempt to leave your body on your own for cheap thrills. There are many dangers and traps out there as there are on this planet if you don't know your way around. Many people have found trouble venturing into these areas alone. If you are a sincere seeker after the truth and wish to know more about your own existence and the totality of the universes, then you'd best call on a Master that you can trust to guide and protect you through these lower worlds such as those previously mentioned—Jesus, Buddha, Zoroaster, Moses, Krishna, Mohammed or some of the great yogis. These Masters can only bring you as far as they themselves can go, which is a long distance into the spiritual realms that lie within the worlds of duality, the negative and positive. No one can lead you through the void into the Soul plane and the pure positive God worlds except an ECK Master. Beyond the void lie endless worlds that are pure and beautiful. There is no negativity there. These are worlds beyond anything one can imagine and they are filled with the Light and Sound of heavenly, heavenly music. Many of us have traveled to these areas under the guidance of one of the ECK Masters, either in the dream state or while daydreaming or during some forms of meditation. We do not always bring the memory of our journey back with us because the mind and the emotions are limited and often cannot handle what has happened to us, or I should say for us. I was complaining that I had no recall of some of my experiences the way some of my friends did, though I knew I was having them. The next morning I woke up with the exact memory of what had occurred while my body was asleep and I was out galavanting. All day I had a smile on my face and was unable to work. All I kept doing was remembering and feeling good and grinning like an idiot. My little voice said to me, now you know why you don't have the memory as some of your friends—you just can't handle it. Then I was able to accept it and be thankful I could get some work done in the days that followed. We do manage to keep the experience, however, through Soul where all of our experiences are stored. Soul resides on the Soul Plane, the beginning of the pure worlds. We each have this connection if we choose to use it. Many of us do remember the experience and bring it back to the rest of our bodies and our mental awareness, and we are never again the same, but begin to struggle to return over and over again into these worlds of Divine Love and beauty and still manage to maintain a balance with our feet firmly planted in the garden, at the kitchen sink, the tractor or the typewriter. There is no way we as individuals can contain all the Divine Love that has poured through us in these states of consciousness. So, when we come back into our bodies as the alarm or the telephone rings, we have all of this to pour out into the world for others to share. We don't have to die to go to heaven, but we do need courage to travel the unknown. We also need to take a Master along with us, or rather, be sure a Master takes us.

One way to do this is to ask one. Either one that you know or you can ask Spirit or God or any of the higher forces you are comfortable with to guide you. If you are sincere in your quest for spiritual unfoldment it will occur.

Many people that are dissatisfied with their lives and don't know why, are looking for something and they don't know what, have traveled to one of these faraway places and experienced bliss unavailable here on this planet. These people may have had the experience in the dream state, but forgotten the dream, while the memory lingers in Soul. It is Soul that is driving them to search, to remember to return to the gifts of God and the gifts that the individual can give to the world. One does not have to even have heard of the ancient path of Eckankar to have been taken by an ECK Master to the higher worlds. They love to take anyone who is ready.

When we realize there are many planes of existence and that we each have a body to correspond to each of the lower planes like the right attire for the right climate, we begin to understand the value of solitude. I wish to make the point here that we do not have any bodies beyond the Soul body. We don't need a body at all to travel the Pure Positive God Worlds, the worlds beyond the void, because the Pure Positive God Worlds are beyond time, space, energy and matter. We don't even travel to these worlds because there is no such thing as travel beyond where time or space, matter or energy do not exist. We simply are. We simply experience these higher worlds by turning our attention to them and with the help of an ECK Master, tuning in and being there. It is very subtle compared to the coarse vibration we are used to on the physical plane, but it is more real than reality as we know it, and every bit more beautiful.

Back to the desire for solitude. As children we spent many hours out of the physical body and operating on another plane. We may have looked like we were "all there" or just "spacing out," going round and round on the floor with our little tiny trucks or rocking a doll to sleep, but even though we looked like that was what we were doing, we were often experiencing other planes of existence and the unearthly colors, beauty, adventure and wisdom to be found there. Most of us never really knew we were any place other than the little chair or the living room floor, basically for our own protection necessary at the time, but we brought back with us a certain knowingness we later discovered we had, having no idea how we knew such things mysteriously or superstitiously. These little adventures that we have can be across the town, state or nation as well as into other planets and other universes. What we experience, the mind can't digest and it becomes excited about concepts like deja vu and cosmic consciousness and such. Once we learn how to "Soul travel" we can be aware of so much of our reason for being here at all, and even our reason for death. Life becomes a brand new thing. Many will call daydreaming an escape. My parents and my teachers were always snapping their fingers at me as a child. But why not take a little side trip away from the turnips you don't feel like eating, instead of staring begrudgingly into them, or while sitting in the dentist's waiting room or inside on a rainy day with no other kids to play with. And for us, it is an escape from the round-and-roundness, from the what's-it-all-aboutness only to learn perhaps, some of what it is all about, which is a lot more than getting born, growing up, falling in love, having children, bringing home the bacon, or getting old and dying. It is about the immortality of each and every one of us and the individual discovery process.

Most of us need to be shown or need to have truth condoned by science. But science is only a measure of the physical reality. How do we know then? We know because each one of us is complete within ourselves. Each one of us contains all truth. WE ARE TRUTH. Each one of us has to find it for ourselves, brave it for ourselves, prove it to ourselves. Although our minds have been trained to disapprove, disagree, and distrust that which it cannot understand, we are equipped to break through those limitations if we choose to use the tools at hand.

My friend Ruth says every time she has to make a decision on something, there is an internal board meeting that convenes. All the members being parts of herself always disagree with each other and she can't decide on anything because she doesn't know which of herselves to listen to. Psychiatry might have a name for it, but these things are not always what they seem. Ruthie is actually getting close. She has realized the different parts of herself and knows there is conflict. Many people are simply tuned in to their emotional body or their mental body and move right along with that voice or that part of themselves. When self-awareness begins to happen and the other parts of ourselves begin to awaken, it gets more difficult because it is not always consciously that we recognize and use the other parts of ourselves. This brings about confusion. Often people in this stage of awareness get frightened. Before they were so strong and clear, and now they can't even make a decision. It looks to them and maybe even others, that they are "losing it."

There isn't much support out there in the mental health area because the spiritual life is not understood and if an individual is open enough to question, they usually consult one of the "experts": priests, rabbis, ministers, etc. who only give part of the picture. Maybe because they only know that much or maybe because the truth is a controlled secret, privy only to the "religious hierarchy." I can't say. It is not a contradiction that I speak of the great teachers of the world, Jesus, Buddha, etc. and then in the same breath refer to the religionists as "experts." It was not Jesus who created Christianity any more than it was Buddha who created Buddhism. These men were too wise for that, for they knew that God was not contained in anything. It was the students or followers of these great men who created the religions, and the religionists who passed it down century after century, losing essence with each day. Through guilt and fear the churches of the world try to keep a hold on their people and continually the people leave, for the knowingness, the God within.

The strange thing is that many of these people who begin to recognize different aspects of themselves, do not realize that they are progressing, growing, developing and unfolding.

Because it doesn't do us any good at all in our daily

lives to be unable to make a decision, we must begin to focus on identifying which of the voices is speaking and which we choose to listen to. Since discovering this, I am becoming at home with all of my bodies, although I still don't have them lined up in perfect balance yet. I do, however, have a harmony within which continues to improve with my spiritual exercises and I am beginning to recognize what level I am coming from, what body I am using; physical, emotional, causal, mental, etheric or Soul. What I'm leaning towards here is keeping tuned into Soul as much as I can, and let It be my guide, going right back to the reality of Spirit or the little inner voice. There are times, of course, that I wish to indulge myself in some way and not listen, and when I choose to do this I must be ready to accept whatever responsibility goes along with it. It's really quite simple, and when we boil it all down, everything really is OUR OWN CHOICE.

chapter eight

# TAKE YOUR SPACE
## It Belongs to You

The day I learned that I didn't have to do anything I didn't want to was a day for celebration. I was at a group picnic and everyone was playing ball and I didn't want to; it took me years to find out I didn't have to. With everyone's coaxing and teasing, if we don't, we feel like a "poor sport." What in the world is a poor sport anyway? Ron was the one who first let me off the hook into understanding that I could "just be" and it was O.K. If I didn't want to go somewhere others wanted me to go, I would feel obligated if I couldn't find a good excuse, as if they would suffer without my being there.

I'm not talking about major events, or responsibilities. I'm speaking of those little obligations or niceties that people bestow on one another; volunteer committees for jobs that must get done for the benefit of school, church, various organizations, or quasi-important social events. If you really don't want to do it, don't. Somebody else will. Sounds cold? It might just be the thing they are looking for at this point, so why should you take it on? When I accepted a time-consuming volunteer job one time, the person who had been there before me said, "Do it as long as it feels right to you and not any more. You are filling a hole and no one else can fill it while it's full. When you're ready to step aside someone will be there to jump in." This made me feel great, and easy about accepting the job. Now if this doesn't happen and no one wants to take over, consider the importance of it in the first place. Perhaps no one cares about the survival of the project, the program or the event. It's not benefitting enough in numbers, and perhaps a different effort would prove more beneficial. If you have a vision, however, that what you're doing needs *you* to take form, then go with it, but enjoy it. The creative process is birthing something you feel is valuable. Love your "baby." If it's not that way then just let it go.

All I'm saying here is to consider these things. Be careful not to automatically take things on because people expect you to be able to handle it so that they can stop looking around for someone else. It's like that old saying "give it to the busiest person and you know it'll get done." It probably will, until that person finally gets angry, or in all her gratuitous efficiency, has a nervous breakdown. You don't have to be superwoman. So choose, choose, choose! Discriminate. Be aware of where your life is going. All these little things make up your life.

We become so busy at certain stages that if we let it, we'd have no time to lay in the sun or speak to the stars.

# HOW EVERYTHING HAPPENS
## (Based on a Study of the wave)

                                        happen.
                                   to
                                up
                        stacking
                           is
                    something
When nothing is happening

When it happens
            something
                    pulls
                        back
                        not
                        to
                        happen.
When                        has happened.
     pulling back      stacking up
            happens

      has happened                        stacks up.
When it         something            nothing
                    pulls back while

Then nothing is happening.
                        happens.[1]
                        and
                    forward
                pushes
             up
        stacks
    something
Then

---

[1]May Swenson, *New and Selected Things Taking Place*
(Massachusetts: 1978).

The friends I see now all understand about time, so I don't have to think of excuses not to be with them. There is just love and that stays. Sometimes we see each other. Sometimes we don't. Be sure you see the distinction here between taking responsibility vs. obligation to please everyone but yourself.

The more one sets one's self up socially, the harder it is to put controls on. It is because the more you're seen out at events, the more invitations you get, and the more your door is open, the more people will come through. In Maine, people were constantly dropping in. I was weaving, Ron was woodworking. Guys would come over to talk about transmissions and women would bring kids. We had to put ourselves in exile. No drop ins. Sunday was open. Sunday there was food and conversation. Very homey and country, but because we both worked at home it wasn't understood that we were serious. That we needed hours and solitude. Company, coffee klatches and committee meeting will become consuming and there will be no time for your intellectual life, your family life, your private life. There will be no time to see the wind move the cloud. Find the balance for yourself.

"And to speak of solitude again, it becomes always clearer that this is at bottom not something that one can take or leave. We are solitary. We may delude ourselves and act as though this were not so. That is all. But how much better it is to realize that we are so, yes, even to begin by assuming it. We shall indeed turn dizzy then; for all points upon which our eye has been accustomed to rest are taken from us, there is nothing near any more and everything far is infinitely far. A person removed from his own room, almost without preparation and transition, and set upon the height of a great mountain range, would feel something of the sort: an unparalleled insecurity, an abandonment to something inexpressible would almost annihilate him. He would think himself falling or hurled out into space, or exploded into a thousand pieces: what a monstrous lie his brain would have to invent to catch up with and explain the state of his senses! So for him who becomes solitary all distances, all measures change; of these changes many take place suddenly, and then, as with the man on the mountaintop, extraordinary imaginings and singular sensations arise that seem to grow out beyond all bearing. But it is necessary for us to experience that too. We must assume our existence as broadly as we in any way can; everything, even the unheard-of, must be possible in it. That is at bottom the only courage that is demanded of us: to have courage for the most strange, the most singular and the most inexplicable that we may encounter. That mankind has in this sense been cowardly has done life endless harm: the experiences that are called "visions," the whole so-called "spirit-world," death, all those things that are so closely akin to us, have by daily parrying been so crowded out of life that the senses with which we could have grasped them are atrophied. To say nothing of God."[2]

There are times we get lost in ourselves. There are other times when we get lost from ourselves. We have to find a balance and both of those things are

[2]Rainer Maria Rilke, *Letters to a Young Poet* (New York: 1963), pp. 66, 67.

necessary at different times. If you haven't thought of a centering method yet, experiment. It's easy to do. Try different sounds; a song, a scat, a chant, maybe your own name, something that calms you, strengthens you...You can even try a vision, a scene from your past, even a color will do. Close your eyes for a moment and center, then you can enter anywhere. Plant an iris, drive a Porsche, raise a pig, build a moon-watching platform.

If we have a problem it helps us to look at it from another perspective. Instead of looking at it from the corner of the room, look at it from the ceiling. Just change your vantage point and watch your problem dissolve.

Don't leave your own thoughts for someone else's. Try to maintain the balance with what you know within yourself and yet remain open to all that is around you. This is from an essay by Alan Watts, called, "Planting Seeds and Gathering Fruit":

"The perfect Way is without difficulty.
Save that it avoids picking and choosing.
Only when you stop liking and disliking
Will all be clearly understood...

Be not concerned with right or wrong.
The conflict between right and wrong
Is the sickness of the mind.[3]"

This idea is admirable, but I could never live it. To me it felt like some far away magical enlightenment would have to take place before I really knew. But no...Enlightenment is a step by step procedure and can't be studied...all that can be studied are the "keys." Then, suddenly you catch the light as if it were a ball. This doesn't mean you can keep it though,

---

[3]Alan Watts, *Does It Matter?* (New York: 1971), p. 109.

for it will surely slip away. But remember that you had it once so let it be a knowingness within and you'll have it always.

Paul Twitchell (from *Anitya*) IWP Publishing, says, "Stop talking, stop thinking and there is nothing you will not understand."[4]

zigzagging low
over petal strewn fields
two finch on the wind.

---

[4]Paul Twitchell, *Anitya* (California: 1969).

If we listen we will not have to ask.
If we listen we will find ourselves
at the center of the entertainment.[1]

---

[1]M. C. Richards, *Centering* (Connecticut: 1961).

## chapter nine

# COMMUNICATION AND CREATIVITY
## The Blue Within

## COMMUNICATE
### COMMUNICATE
### COMMUNICATE
### COMMUNICATE
### COMMUNICATE

with your mother, your friend, your kid, your spouse, your colleague and yourself. This does not just mean talk. This means more like LISTEN and not just listen to the words but listen to the HEART. People often cannot say what they are feeling because they often do not know what they are feeling. It's not clear to them. Many of us are not as in touch with ourselves as we would like to be. We'll walk out of a meeting or a party feeling confused and depressed or like a can of worms has just crawled over us and not know why. What happened? Were we put under subtle attack, the subject of someone's negative thought forms? Be aware when you feel your energy dropping in the presence of someone—move away from them or surround yourself with imaginary mirrors so instead of penetrating you, their negativity is reflected back at them.

Listening with our whole selves is important in any kind of relationship. It means talk as well because we have to let people know where we are coming from so that we cannot blame them if they don't come through. If we expect something from a person and it doesn't happen, it may be because that person does not know that we expect that of them, so we can't get mad at them. Just check in and let them know what it is that we want from them. They will either be willing or unwilling to give it, but in either case, we will know how they feel and won't have to sulk around in a bunch of gray vagueries.

Remember the little things that are easy to do but that are so important to a relationship. Do them to feed that relationship. Make scrumptious muffins for the weekend if you are not going to be around, buy someone a bar of special soap, a single flower, a box of crayolas even if they are 43 years old. Everyone loves crayolas from the fondest of childhood memories. Magic markers have almost rendered them obsolete.

Sometimes I can go for days with so many things on my mind and living within my own world that I don't really make contact. Suddenly it dawns on me that the happiness level has dropped around the house and I need just give a person a smile, a hug, a loving lingering glance and SPARK! Everything is all right again. It does a lot for me too.

Sometimes if I'm over involved for a few days and my attention is far away from the people I live with, I try to remember to tell them I'm in that place and please excuse me while I live there for awhile, getting things done that don't necessarily include them, but that I'll be back soon. Then when I am back, I make sure to let them know I am back and that it's neat things don't go weird while I am "gone." Just keeping those around you informed as to your comings and goings so that when you're not particularly friendly to your co-worker for a few days, she doesn't think it's her, but knows that it's you and your preoccupation. We are all so sensitive that if your behavior on the job or at home suddenly changes, it puts them to wondering. Many people, many you would least suspect, need recognition for the job they've done and reassurance that you're still with them. A co-worker of mine called me this morning to get my reaction to the meeting we co-chaired. This is a very vivacious and intelligent woman who is not afraid to speak her mind. She called this morning to see what I thought of the meeting and particularly, her presentation, although she didn't say so. I thought it was obviously a productive and enthusiastic session. She said, "I know you would never guess it, but I'm really very insecure and I need a lot of feedback, so from now on..."

Telling one of my kids out of the blue that I'm proud of them is an amazing thing. Not after a good report card, a game or a recital, but just out of the blue. They usually say, "Really, how come?" and I just list all the things I love about them. People like to know they are doing okay. If there is a disagreement and one of the kids wants to do something I don't want them to do, I usually say no. When they start to argue and ask me why not and I don't know why not but I just don't want them to, I tell them that. I have learned to say, "I don't know. I just don't feel good about it and I trust my feelings even though I can't explain it, it's my job not to let you go." Said with love and understanding and empathizing instead of getting argumentative and defensive, she has no choice but to accept it. She may be angry with me but I don't allow myself to get into her anger, and in the long run I know she has received several important lessons. One is trusting your feelings, being firm in your belief even though it had no logical justification, and doing your job as a parent even though it's sometimes a lot easier to let them talk you into their thing, and that you can also understand her feelings of anger/disappointment. Oftentimes, I've seen my kids argue and argue until they could see it was useless and then warm right up and settle down into something else. This is an exercise in the practice of responsibility, compassion and detachment.

To get back to listening, I made a shocking

discovery about myself while doing the research for this book. I interviewed a lot of people on a lot of issues on a cassette recorder. I'd come home and play the tape and see where I missed someone's entire meaning because I was so busy interacting, (talking myself), looking for the next question to ask them instead of really hearing what they were saying. This was especially true when I met with a group of black women to discuss the survival issue they had to deal with while growing up. When I got home and played the tape back I could hear myself trying very hard to find similarities and yet, their issues were indeed different. Their survival forms were multi-faceted, and I was looking for common ground which was contradictory to the whole reason I was interviewing them in the first place. It was indeed a lesson.

### More on Listening...

I am able to pinpoint the frustration now after having sat with Margaret and Hillary having wine last night—what it is in the midst of these deep, self-searching dialogues that leaves me confused. Last night, speaking on the point of sisters, I spoke of the divorce between Nancy and myself and how we're now reunited. Hillary asked, "But did you declare your divorce to each other?" I said, "Yes." She said, "That's very brave of you. I can't do that. It's easier for me to gulp and look away." For me that was frustrating as I wanted to get on with the point—the "good stuff," but I was kept prisoner as if I was reluctant to give myself credit for bravery. "But it wasn't brave," I said. "It was easy. It was survival. It was self-defense. Some things are painful and hard and when I do those I'm brave. For you, this would be brave."

"But you are being unfair to yourself," they insisted, keeping me from going on to the original point. Obviously, this had now become the point.

I stopped and listened and heard where they were and what they were trying to get me to do. "Oh," I said, "it wasn't always easy. Starting from square one, everything had to be begun, tried, learned and conquered, so, yes, at one time I had to face that issue, but no longer, not for centuries. Why keep going back, collecting your credit slips? Why not start from now?"

They were relieved, either that I had acknowledged that at one time it had been hard or yes, I did deserve the credit for bravery and would indeed accept it.

Is this a detainment?

I realized I had wrongly assumed that we were starting from the same place.

## The Secret

Two girls discover
The secret of life
in a sudden line of
poetry.

I, who don't know the
secret wrote
the line. They
told me

(Through a third person)
They had found it
but not what it was
not even

what line it was. No doubt
by now, more than a week
later, they have forgotten
the secret,

the line, the name of
the poem. I love them
for finding what
I can't find,

and for loving me
for the line I wrote,
and for forgetting it
so that

a thousand times, till death
finds them, they may
discover it again, in other
lines

in other
happening. And for
wanting to know it,
for

assuming there is
such a secret, yes
for that
most of all.[2]

We can't condemn a writer for not meeting our needs, because their writing is probably directed to a consciousness other than our own or maybe not even directed. Maybe it just pours through us leaving us untouched on its way to someone else. We have to find the writings directed to us and in the same way we can direct our efforts from where we are coming from, and those who need to hear what we have to say will be the ones we have said it for. We don't always know our audience. We rarely know another person's consciousness, so all we can do is let it come through "out there," sow the seeds and let them grow where they will. We are all students. We are all teachers.

When I was a little girl, my father terrorized me. He held love over my head like a candy bar. I was always striving for his approval and when I got it it was delicious, his love seemed so great. When he was

    [2]Denise Levertov-Goodman, *O Taste and See* (New York: 1964).

disapproving, it was demoralizing and sickening and I could never come to my own defense. I couldn't talk and I hated myself for just sitting there while tears soaked my face. The frustration of not being able to confront him with my point of view drove me to writing. I made lists of all the ways he was unfair and all the things that he was wrong about and even if I didn't always show them to him, I sorted things out in my own head and didn't feel so inadequate. I had the lists stacked in the corner of my drawer as ammunition if I ever needed them, and I did on occasion. It would have been far better, of course, if I could have had a verbal exchange, but our relationship was so emotionally charged I couldn't think straight in those situations. It's a good technique as a last resort when you're involved with a domineering person, just a sane and simple letter will do.

Cable TV is a wide-open forum if you have something to say. There is still time available and there is equipment for use. Bring your ideas and creations to the new station near you or investigate starting your own. It is a great opportunity to get some quality viewing into the living room and can even be the beginning of an exciting career.

> Right inner talk forms the
> successful image. What is
> called creativeness is only becoming
> aware of what already is. Nothing
> is ever created, it is only manifested.[3]

---

[3]Darwin Gross, *Gems of Soul* (California: 1980), p. 37.

# CREATIVITY

Everyone is a creator. By merely having a thought, we create a future condition. Everyone, however, does not have the potential to make art. What art and beauty are have long been an issue of debate. The following is the decision I have arrived at after spending a lifetime pondering the question.

The artist is one who inspires, moves the viewer "in spirit" to a higher state of consciousness, one who cannot help being an artist despite public opinion and the economic gamble, one who lives for and through his art.

There have been those through the ages who have been able to portray the way things are in a most excruciatingly accurate way. Statements of war, hunger, and confusion have been made by many through time and these expressions can be valuable statements acting as alarm clocks for that particular civilization to awaken. The world lives in fear, anger, lust and turmoil. It is in us and all around us. Art works to bring us from misery and mediocrity into the beautiful. It reminds us of the magic around us and especially within us. The way light acts upon our very beings, and sound as well, for every color has a special sound, and being a vibration so does every form. Light and sound in its purest sense is heaven on earth. It lifts us out of ourselves, beyond our senses. It "inspires." And as artists, when we manifest these moments, these sounds, colors, shapes and movements, it doesn't come from us. The process of creating removes us from ourselves and if we step out of the way, we find the image, vision, vibration coming down and out through us. Being the instrument, the vehicle, to bring it down, we know the ecstasy of those precise moments of manifestation, the energy coming through us onto the page, a gift to us, and having done our part, from us. As well as the ecstasy as artists, we know all too well the agony of emptiness, the spinning of the mental wheels in longing for this essence once again. And, if we are not patient, not careful, we are in danger of trying to be clever, a symptom every artist needs to watch out for. It is all too easy to become popular with a little skill and cleverness, but is it art?

"We come to know in art work that we do not clearly know where we will arrive in our work, although we set the compass, our vision; that we are led, in going along, by material and work process. We have plans and blueprints, but the finished work is still a surprise. We learn to listen to voices: to the yes or no of our material, our tools, our time. We come to know that only when we feel guided by them our work takes on form and meaning, that we are misled when we follow only our will. All great deeds have been achieved under a sense of guidance. We learn courage from art work. We have to go where no one was before us. We are alone and we are responsible for our actions. Our solitariness takes on religious character: this is a matter of my conscience and me."[4]

If we are skilled, if we love and work, suffer it, knead it, contemplate it, practice and torture ourselves to perfection over it, over the mastery of the media we choose to use, and are then able to step aside for it to come through, then we are the artist, the manifestor, the creator, the one who has seen the essence in a thing, a sky, a pear, a tree. The artist, one who has seen the essence of it, the energy of it, the spirit in it and has managed to translate that into a picture for the viewer, is able to experience that same

---

[4]Anni Albers, *On Designing* (Connecticut: 1943), p. 31.

essence. As one who has brought the experience of the being of the pear onto paper, into a picture, the manifestor is able to draw out the life of the pear for the viewer, while still leaving the pear very much alive, a gift to the viewer. Or a woodworker, seeing the joy in a piece of maple and creating a chair that makes one smile, manifesting a piece of furniture that has a presence other than just something to sit on, but a presence that has life of its own, to be and live as a friendly object in harmony with the room it sits in.

Excerpts from "Reminiscences" by Wassily Kandinsky[5]

"Here is a world which, derived from the desires of pictures already painted, was also determined and created through accidents, through the puzzling play of forces alien to the artist. And I owe much to these accidents; they have taught me more than any teacher or master. Many an hour I studied them with love and admiration. The pallette which consists of the elements mentioned, which in itself is a "work" and often more beautiful than many another work, should be valued for the pleasures which it offers. It sometimes seemed to me that the brush, which with unyielding will tore pieces from this living color creation, evoked a musical sound in this tearing process. Sometimes I heard a hissing of the colors as they were blending. It was like an experience that one could hear in the secret kitchen of the alchemist, cloaked in mystery."

---

[5]Wassily Kandinsky, "Reminiscences," *Modern Artists on Art: Ten Unabridged Essays,* by Robert L. Herbert (New Jersey: 1964), p. 20.

"With the years, I have now learned somewhat to control this creative power. I have trained myself—not simply to let myself go, but to bridle the power working within me, to guide it. With the years I have understood that with a pounding heart, with a straining breast (and thus aching ribs later), and with tension in my whole body cannot suffice. It can, however, only exhaust the artist, not his work. The horse bears the rider with strength and speed. But the rider guides the horse. Talent carries the artist to great heights with strength and speed, but the artist guides his talent. This is the element of the "conscious," the "calculating" in his work or whatever one wants to call it. The artist must know his talent through and through and like a smart businessman, leave not the least bit unused and forgotten; instead he must exhaust and develop every particle to the maximum possible for him."

"Entirely without consciousness, I steadily absorbed impressions, sometimes so intensively and incessantly that I felt as if my chest were cramped and my breathing difficult. I became so overtired and overstuffed that I often thought with envy of clerks who were permitted and able to relax completely after their day's work. I longed for dull witted rest, for eyes which Boecklin called "porters eyes." I had, however, to see without pause. A few years ago I suddenly noticed that this ability had diminished. At first I was horrified, but later I understood that the powers that made continuous observation possible were being channeled in another direction through my more highly developed ability to concentrate, and could accomplish other things now more necessary to me. My capacity for absorbing myself in the spiritual life of art (and thus too, of my soul) increased so greatly that I often passed external phenomena without noticing them, something that could never have happened before."

There are those who do not have to struggle for mastery, who do not seem to be starting from scratch, where the skill and beauty just seem to flow out of them with apparently little effort. This is most likely a continuity carried over from past lifetimes of study.

If we, however, labor over every line, shadow, leaf or twig, if we get so absorbed in the subject with our minds, we forget to let go, to edit, to flow, we end up with an accurate portrayal of the park floor, but what does that do for us?

I always knew that much of the creative process had to do with walking back and forth with a mug of coffee between two hands, staring. Great breakthroughs have been made away from the desk. Much of this book is being written with a notebook on the counter, a ready cassette player by the sink and my hands in dishwater.

A self portrait I once made called Self Portrait in the Laundromat, was a dark circle of tumbling clothes and a faint reflection of my face. How many wondrous winter nights with steamed up windows I stared aimlessly in the quiet of that moving, tumbling circle.

Spacing out is a process. It is a means to an end. A step for some.

Without spacing out we'd have fewer poems, less inventions, a scarcity of art and no saints at all. We'd have no wisdom, no time to see. When I talk about spacing out it also includes spacing in. Marshall MacLuhan said the environment becomes invisible. That is a spiritual waste.

The sun settles reflected by the ice, warming
the crevices of the hard, cold, rock and so
here I am again with me...and you...
takes awhile to get used to
The phone lurks in the corner
the car ready
yet paradise is right here. I never knew that
    frozen lakes sing.
What else is there about this I do
    not know?
Wonder is a very fitting key to the riddles of
    the universe.


If we know the flow, and know we are the instrument, the manifestor, but don't perfect our skills for
translating our vision, if we don't stretch daily so our
leg will lift into that perfect arch, or our arm will
sweep the page with graceful ease, we cannot translate
the vision, we have no rhythm. What we experience
does not speak to another and that again is not art. It
is true that some of the responsibility is in the eye of
the beholder. We as observer are responsible for the
ability to perceive, but if it is not there, it just is not
there. As the artist, when we work our disciplines and
then step aside and let spirit direct us, we can then
give our visions earthly form.
    One night a long time ago I went to Cambridge
alone. Going alone was hard for me then but it was
my way of forcing me to find and be myself, whoever
and whatever that was. At times like these I used to
dress up differently, try on different images to see
what fit and go out into the world. In the past, I had
always surrounded myself with friends and family,
untrusting of the possibility of my own existence. It
was an unconscious effort to become strong and to
find those things within myself that went unnoticed in

the company of others. At the time I was studying painting in Boston and went across the river to hear Joseph Albers, the great colorist and painter. He gave a talk accompanied by a slide show and with each new slide I became more and more alive. I was beginning to see in a new and vital way, colors in squares placed against each other in a way that made them new, made them sound. I danced in ecstasy within myself, returning home across the river, seeing nothing, no buses, no buildings, or people walking. I saw only a brilliant blue square, vibrating in my eye. Ecstatic to be lifted so far out of my physical reality, so glad to be losing all consciousness of self for something so abstract. I laughed aloud imagining what might people think if they knew I was pregnant with a vibrant blue square. I have always been grateful to Joseph Albers for that gift and later as I began seeing, I also began discovering others who spoke the same language; Alexie Jawlenski, Gabrielle Munter, and Wassily Kandinsky and many others—Matisse, Monet and Paul Klee. It wasn't till a few months ago that I discovered that Kandinsky was a writer as well and in the same way his paintings touched me so did his words. Different art speaks to different consciousness and well it is we have no measure of beauty. Art is a personal experience for the doer as well as the viewer.

"After a silence, in which were gentle dreams, I asked of her: What thing is this beauty? For people differ in its defining and their knowledge thereof as they contend one with another in praise and love of it."

And she answered, "It is that which draws your spirit. It is that which you see and makes you to give rather than receive. It is that thing you feel when hands are stretched forth from your depths. It is that which the body reckons a trial and the spirit a bounty. It is the link between joy and sorrow. It is all that you perceive hidden and unknown and hear silent. It is a force that begins in the holy of holies of your being and ends in that place beyond your visions..."[6]

An example of the subjectivity of Beauty is the following from Alice B. Toklas.

"Of the final falling out, Alice admitted that Gertrude had compared Madame Matisse's beauty to that of a horse, but she was surprised, she concluded, that Matisse did not think a horse beautiful."[7]

"When man no longer experiences, the organs of his inner life wither away. Alone or in herds he goes on binges of violence and destruction. Looking and seeing both start with sense perception, but there the similarity ends. When I 'look' at the world and label its phenomena, I made immediate choices, instant appraisals—I like or dislike, I accept or reject, what I look at, according to its usefulness to the 'ME'...THIS ME THAT I IMAGINE MYSELF TO BE, AND THAT I TRY TO IMPOSE ON OTHERS. The purpose of 'looking' is to survive, to cope, to manipulate, to discern what is useful, agreeable, or threatening to the ME, what enhances or what diminishes the ME. This we are trained to do from our

---

[6]*The Kahlil Gibran Diary for 1980*, "Beauty" (New York: 1980).

[7]Linda Simon, *The Biography of Alice B. Toklas* (Avon Books).

first day. When, on the other hand, I SEE—suddenly I am all eyes, I forget this ME, am liberated from it and dive into the reality of what confronts me, become part of it, participate in it. I no longer label, no longer choose. ("Choosing is the sickness of the mind," says a sixth century Chinese sage.) It is in order to really SEE, to SEE ever deeper, ever more intensely, hence to be fully aware and alive, that I draw what the Chinese call 'The Ten Thousand Things' around me. Drawing is the discipline by which I constantly rediscover the world. I have learned that what I have not drawn, I have never really seen, and when I start drawing an ordinary thing, I realize how extraordinary it is. Sheer miracle."[8]

Billie Holiday was an artist. She sang the blues. The blues heal the astral (emotional) body which is why there has always been a form of the blues in all cultures at all times. It is no coincidence that the black people tuned into the blues, with so many wounds to be healed. Billie Holiday is a healer and an artist. Try singing the blues when you're down and watch yourself rise.

Paul Klee in an essay called "Schopferische Konfession" writes:

"Before, things which were visible on earth were described, things which either people were glad to see or would have wished to see. Now, the reality of visible things has spread, and there is a widespread, absolute conviction that, in relation to the whole of the universe, what we can see is only an isolated part of it and there are other infinite truths,

---

[8]Frederick Franck, *The Zen of Seeing* (New York: 1973).

hidden and greater."

And from his diary on July 17, 1917:
"All that is transitory is only allegory. What
we see is a proposal, a possibility, a help.
Real truth lies on an invisible foundation."

At the end of the essay Klee wrote:
"Every energy demands a complimentary
one in order to achieve a state of stillness in
itself, strung as it is between opposing
forces. In the end what is created is a cosmos
of abstract formal elements in union with
concrete beings or abstract things like numbers or letters, a cosmos, so like the great
creation itself that sometimes all it needs is a
breath to make it become religious expression, the true religion; art behaves symboli-
cally towards creation. Art is thus a symbol,
as earthly things are a cosmic symbol."

In 1918, Klee wrote of his work:
"Behind the variety of interpretations there
is a final secret, and the light of the intellect
is wretchedly put out."[9]

Klee, working from the higher worlds and bringing
his vision into physical manifestation was forced to
begin to study his own system upon acceptance of a
teaching position at the famous Bauhaus so that he
himself could understand and pass on to his students
this process that he was using. His efforts were
involved not only with teaching his students art, but
the opening up of a new reality for individual explora-
tion.

Truth is simple and certainly doesn't need to be put

---

[9]Hans L. Jaffe and A. Busignani, *Klee* (New York: 1972).

into words arranged by me if they are already well arranged by somebody else. Here is something by Martha Graham.

> "There is a vitality, a life force, an energy, a quickening that is translated through you into actions, and because there is only one of you in all of time, this expression is unique. And if you block it, it will never exist through any other medium and be lost. It is not your business to determine how good it is, nor how valuable, nor how it compares with other expressions. It is your business to keep it yours, clearly and directly, to keep the channel open. You do not even have to believe in yourself or your work. You have to keep open and aware to the urges that motivate you. Keep the channel open."[10]

---

[10]Martha Graham (Original source unknown by author. Handed down from friend to friend through papers carried in wallets).

"Don't look at the pitcher, but what it contains. Sometimes a new pitcher is full of old wine, and an old pitcher is empty of even new wine."

Rabbi Yehuda Hanassi
—excerpt from the Mishna

For Adam

Somersault boy in blue
sprawled on the flowered rug
I throb to floppy dark dreams
   of your hair
And the vulnerable world of your eyes
Unaware of my mother mush
You belong to you.

## chapter ten

# DETACHMENT
## Parenting and Letting Go

I am 44 today, and I have earned it. It seems old to the young and young to the old. For me, it's just right. It's where I belong.

Abe Lincoln once said something like—"after forty every man should be responsible for his own face." Upon scrutiny, I see upon mine two definite creases running slantwise from the end of my nose down the sides of the mouth, my eyes shine and my skin is pink and glowing. I accept these creases that came and deepened with each season. I know their birth from hearty hugs and deep felt anger, from frigid nights under blankets listening to far away cars, waiting for a child's footstep on the stairs. The creases come from the joy of love, the waiting for lovers, the search for God. But I like the face, remembering the dark shining eyes and remembering not to think of the fantasy ladies in Mademoiselle and Cosmo. The richness of experience, which takes time and knowing that the rough times that await are just a step, another test, to be followed by its opposite, the reward, the balance, the complete cycle.

During the hard and ugly times, the frightened times, it's hard to remember there's more happening than the table not getting set, the cat poop on the floor, the note from the school on tardiness and the mountain of unpaid bills, but there is more, and if our attention can be placed into our own most beautiful of places, if we can again remember each moment is a test, then we can laugh and rise above it. This rising above it is something I always had a hard time with, so pure and pompous, but it really is a knack. What's the worst that can happen if we leave the mess for half an hour to touch base with the higher force within us. Who knows, there might be a speck of humor in the situation. We always have the choice to be stuck or move on.

The BIG problems, like your husband having an affair or your kid dropping out of school are hard ones. I've had them both and then some. You can only do what you can do. If my husband is naive enough to actually think he's in love with another woman he's just discovered, with long hair and a young body, if he's silly enough to let his ego become flattered, his whole perception become distorted, then who needs him? If he's so insecure, middle aged or not, that flattery can actually pull him away, then I'd show him what he's doing. If he won't look, I'd let him go. But if he is aware he needs these extra strokes from someone else, and at the same time knows what he's got in me, I'll talk to him and more important, listen to him, give him the strokes he needs through his crisis, let him know what is happening as I see it, then let him go. I see no crime in needing more than you've got providing you know what it is you are really doing and providing you don't fall for the illusion of being in "love." The real hurt, I think, for most of us has little to do with sex, but the talk that goes on around it. The thing I hated the most was the thought that everyone knew something that I didn't and the gossip and pity that followed. Often sex is the focal point of the imagination and is really not the issue. For most of us betrayed, it's the fear of emotional entanglement and for the betrayer it's the attention, the thrill of newness and the feeling of worth. Sex is only the instrument for the linkup. If it could be broken down into parts, it would be a lot easier for us to take if one knew what it was we wanted and could become cause, like—I need some fun in my life, some spice without entanglement. I'll find someone looking for the same thing, not one looking for love and protection, rather than having the process an unconscious one and simply allow yourself to float downstream into falling in love. Even though the latter would be more exciting and pleasureful, it would no doubt be more painful in the end.

I have found that over the years, my desire to have a fling never had anything to do with my love for Ron or lack of it or being a sexually frustrated female, but it had to do with the way I felt about myself. The three things necessary for my well-being had to do with: 1. Mothering well 2. Creating in some form—poems, weavings, painting or gardening and 3. Earning. When these three aspects of my life were on low, unbeknownst to me I would begin looking for some excitement, actually looking for some worth through another person. When I found that out, I began looking to myself for fulfillment. Looking to see what needed adjusting within. Needless to say, it was not as much fun. It was hard work, but the benefits far outweigh the losses. First of all, the hard work in itself became the creative aspect, the good mothering naturally began to occur, stability and joy began to fill my being and very importantly, I didn't get tangled up in unnecessary karma. There are times, however, when people do well to end a marriage, where both parties benefit from their new beginning.

Jekyll-Hyde or June Hannah

It took three years
to cause the
transformation

For the strategies
of helplessness
to fall away

Like old skin
Becoming Miss instead
of Mrs. after years

Of fusion is
a change like an
explosion

It takes time to fill
an empty hand
create new feet

to stand. And rise up
taller than you
can on any husband's
shoulders.[1]

There is so much worry over the transition parents
have to make when the kids leave the nest. "What
now" kind of thing. It seems to me that most of us
were people before we had kids and if we continue the
interests we had before, though we may not have the
time to pursue them the way we once did before
becoming parents, we can still keep a thread of continuity going.

When my friend Abby, one of the best painters I
know, became pregnant with her first child I said,
"don't stop, no matter what." She didn't. Now her
kids are in junior high and high school and she is able
to spend many disciplined hours in the studio each
day, working professionally and producing magnifi-
cently. The early years with the babies were, of course,
busy times, but she didn't let go. Though we may not
have time to pursue as we did before we had small
children, we can still maintain an interest or find new
ones, set aside some time for ourselves, our own discipline and enjoyment throughout the child rearing
years.

By the time the kids are gone, although we may
miss the fullness and richness of family and friends,
we begin to welcome the time and the space to pursue

[1] Joan Shapiro, *Coloring Book* (Connecticut: 1978), p. 84.

our interests that have taken a back seat for so long. For one thing, we have rooms to convert and for another, we have fewer housekeeping chores.

The best teaching is by example and if we have interests they automatically get passed on through us. Not only by what we do, but by the fact that we do, that we respect ourselves enough to give to ourselves. It doesn't matter what it is— gardening, community work, school, craft, career, biking, hiking, baking, sailing, fishing, who cares as long as it gives us that spark that keeps us from drudgery, monotony and the "Guiding Light."

To love being a homemaker is one thing—it is rich. To martyr ourselves is another thing and that is poor. The martyrs are never the real saints. Living just for our children or through them is not a measure of real love, but rather a measure of negligence for ourselves. It leaves us without, and dependent and left to sorrow over the trauma of forced retirement. And, more importantly, the lesson of self love and independence has not been provided, but in many instances, a false set of obligations and guilt.

When your child is dropping out of school or is on drugs or whatever, be there for him or her. Listen. Don't judge and don't let your own compassion and understanding get over-powered by society's values. Check your real values against those imposed. When my son at sixteen said he wanted out, my first reaction was "Oh my God, we failed. Where will he go? What will he do? How will he make it?" and the big one— "What will people think?"

First I screamed for five minutes and ranted. Then seeing his frustration, I put my arm around him and we sat down. I talked about the pitfalls, the darkness and the dreams to a boy who had always been smart, but who had always done poorly in school. Having come into this life with wisdom and imagination, he, like many others, was forced to drop his "real self" in order to squeeze into the mold the school system had built by less imaginative minds, and still he didn't fit. I remember in the first grade they were giving tests that Adam scored poorly on. The teachers were treating him like a slow but well-behaved child. I couldn't bear the lie. The PTA had as a guest speaker, one of those gentlemen from the testing industry to tell us all about the benefits of the tests. I confronted him with my thoughts on the power and inadequacy of such tests and spoke of our situation. He said, "it is an unfortunate thing, but we have no way of measuring the intelligence of people like your son. In the trade, we have a name for such people and we call them 'maverick mentality' as they are usually original thinkers, so that a way of measuring them hasn't been invented thus far." Meanwhile, the teachers were not informed of this, I guess, because it would have put a hole in the sales pitch going out all over the country to inadequately measure some of the greatest of our nation's young minds, but as a side effect, these so-called maverick mentalities were being pushed aside as rejects instead of being encouraged to continue thinking originally. Everyone knew that Einstein couldn't make it in school. Well, this was a large part of the painful scholastic (and spilling over into social) history of one of many young people, starting them onto a path of assumed failure. There is much literature on the subject by now and there was a period where humanistic educators began opening up their own schools. Before Adam dropped out, he had the opportunity to attend one for three whole years, but basically all it gave him was permission to be himself. Who that self was at that time was of course pretty vague, and drugs being readily available made it a lot easier for him to avoid being himself, whoever that was.

After three years, he had the total accumulation of one credit, and a question of what grade he was actually in. We made a shot at a regular school with the idea that he was willing to risk humiliation and really try to pull it together even if it meant summer school and staying back. He gave it an honest try, but because of his record, he was treated by the school as one of their more serious delinquents and there wasn't a soul there willing to take him under their wing. They just expected more of the same of his past record and didn't see that he was sick of the situation and really wanted to tackle it. They made it hard for him to be strong, so he left.

He sat around for a week, found himself a job which allowed him to buy all the dope he could use and he did that for six months. All of this time it was painful to watch him come and go, not knowing his whereabouts and trying to deal with our own anger and frustration.

Even though it was a difficult siege because I had allowed his pain to become my pain, gradually I began to see that I had suffered in my own way at his age for having a similar kind of temperament and I had made out okay. I also knew that one day, I didn't know when, but one day I knew his power would emerge. I also began to remember that the worst part for me as I was going through adolescence was watching my parent's fear and heavy, heavy worry, so I learned to hide. I kept my feelings and own inner fears from them as if sharing would make them multiply. So here I was on the flip side of that coin thinking I already went through this once, I'd be a fool to put myself through it again. He then began to see that we did have faith in him and that we knew that sooner or later he would be on his own, beginning to get his act together. Our change in attitude aided in his change. He knew that his self-discipline had to come from him alone and that we had become detached, knowing his experience was his own, knowing that we were there for him with love and support but without any more of our nagging, lectures, contracts and deals. He was responsible to him as we went about our daily business, living and laughing.

At the last possible moment in his second alternative school he managed to qualify for graduation by a tough jury made up of peers, faculty administrators and family. He was lucky to have the opportunity and with great relief and a heartwarming speech, he walked away with a diploma leaving total strangers in tears.

Now at nineteen, he is one of the most independent but giving people I know. Having obtained a year and a half of employment, raises and responsibility, he is now paying for his car, car insurance and night school tuition. He is a nineteen year old with clear goals and high motivation.

The whole point of this tale is to show that had we remained attached, heartached and pushed through this process, we would have ended up with less. Adam's process had to run its own course and our having anguished over it would have only provided a lot of guilt on his part and a lot of misery on ours.

Our job as parents is to guide our children, showing them that they have choices every moment that only they can make and that they alone must take the responsibility for each and every choice. There are many ways to do things and there are skills to be learned in getting by in this world while not being a slave to it.

Once we understand karma and the purpose of each experience, because each experience does have a purpose, it is much easier to operate from beyond the emotional level.

I didn't allow those situations to get me down. I did not take the blame. I didn't feel guilt or inadequacy because I knew I had done my best. I knew I had not copped out on either husband or son. I loved them and wanted things right, but what they did with their own lives was up to them and I had one of my own to live. This is called "letting go." It does work. I found we cannot mold our loved ones into our needs or after the image we choose for them. Life is full of surprises and flexibility, detachment and love help one to meet them.

*Two Premises:*
1. We as Soul, our children and ourselves chose each other to experience for this particular lifetime. We all agreed that we had something to share and learn from each other before Soul ever entered the baby body that came through us as mothers. So it is not by chance nor, hard as it sometimes seems, are we mismatched. It was a covenant made by child and parents as Soul, usually before the birth. The essence of ourselves does not enter the body till birth.
2. This new baby is often a very old Soul, having lived lifetimes, some of them maybe even with you. So, here you are the mother, the instrument for the current manifestation of this human being, now responsible for its protection, guidance and care until the age of 18.

We get surprised at times by the precociousness of our children, but if we pay attention, we'll discover that they have just as much to teach us as we them. It is a mistake to think that because we are older, we are smarter. Often the still unsocialized child is wiser than we, having come freshly from the higher worlds down into the civilization of this confusing planet, earth. As the child progresses in school and in life it is forced to let go of much of its wisdom for a more practical and efficient way of life. Actually, growing up is a de-education process until we as individuals begin to catch on to the fact that there is a bigger picture to this reality than can readily be seen.

Usually when we begin to awaken to this reality, we get little support and few answers to the reasons for our existence, or the meaning of life. Most of us soon give up asking and settle down into the "normal" way of living. Soon our dissatisfaction apathizes and we become involved in the daily business of bringing home the bacon. Some of us, however, cannot give up no matter how hard we try and something in us pushes us on in our search for answers to the thus far unanswerable questions.

We often suffer the fear of maladjustment, dependency on drugs or alcohol or become depressed. We're referred to as discontent, blasphemous, idealistic, spacey, poetic but naive. Some of us, those who share our visions with the "experts" sometimes end up in mental hospitals or suicidal only because the "experts" on religion don't have the answers we're looking for and the "experts" in mental health don't know much about Spirit. So the name calling and the locking us away is merely a method of sweeping a disturbing and unanswerable issue under the rug.

When this is understood by parent and child, there is mutual respect and love which comes with the knowledge of deliberateness and choice. I didn't always know this mentally, although instinctively it's always been with me. This knowledge, however, does not guarantee perpetual bliss and smooth as silk relationships. It does pretty much guarantee love, respect and even trust.

Our job as parents is not to live our children's lives or to make them a reflection of ourselves. Our job is to show them the way to get along in this world. To lay down the guidelines and set up the rules. While they live under our roof, they have certain responsibilities to fulfill. As teenagers, keeping us informed of their whereabouts—checking in—is their responsibility. It is our responsibility to make it clear to them that we are not in fact checking up on them for lack of trust, but rather for our own assurance that they are safe from the world. Kids often think they're indestructible and the "bad things" happen to others. They are often naive about the dangers in the street. This in a way is what gives them the freedom to be confident. However, if they can be taught to be aware without constipating them with fear, both parent and child will benefit.

I still have a tendency when crossing a busy street to block my kids from running into traffic even though they're taller than me. I laugh, remembering riding horses in the California hills. There I'd be on a narrow ridge, steering the horse as if it was a car. Suddenly, realizing the horse wasn't about to commit suicide by wandering off a cliff, it became a lot more fun. Each being is equipped with self-preservation instincts and we do not have to steer our offspring through life. With a little guidance, love and support, they can find their own way.

Yesterday, Lizzie came back from attending her best friend's 16th birthday luncheon in a very fancy restaurant. She was seated at a table of 19 girls, mother, grandmother and father. By the time the melon balls had been cleared away, she found herself in the bathroom crying. A joyful, easy-going person, Lizzie was confused by her own outburst. What she later figured out was that as she sat there, she was overcome by a sudden realization of separateness, despite the love she had for her friend. It was a sudden perception of a difference in values that she recognized, leaving her violently isolated and alone among the gaiety. Sad as she felt she was grateful for the discovery.

"Frequently unexpected behavior and a lack of sharing are signs that our child is working hard to develop an identity separate from ours. Although we may recognize this change as an important stage, it may be difficult to find a comfortable way of living with it."[2]

Saturday night, Ron and I were sitting with some friends at a purple clothed round table, drenched in candlelight and tearing apart Rock Cornish Hens, when we both got drawn into separate conversations. Since many of us were educators as well as parents of teenage and college kids, we found ourselves evaluating the success and/or failure of our kids. Personally I think there is no such thing, but I was surprised when Beverly, sitting to my right said, "Marge, I'm worried about Kim— (her daughter). She's been away at school almost for a year now and still has no idea what she wants to do with her life. I think I gave her double messages all the way through." I said to her, "That happens a lot because you were being honest with her and speaking from wherever you were at that time. Just talk to her now and see if you can deconfuse her and let her know that it was hard for you to be consistent since you were going through so many changes yourself. Tell her that you were being honest and did the best you could. That's all anyone can do." She said, "But I wasn't honest." To this I had no reply. For goodness sake be honest with your kids. People say, "Marge you're so lucky you have such a great relationship with your kids." It's not luck at all. No matter what kind of hell or weirdness Ron and I were going through, we never lied to the kids. They never grew up thinking we were perfect and then having the great disillusion when they reached adolescence. They sometimes learned from our mistakes, sometimes disapproved, but we never lived a lie. When Beverly saw my reaction, she said, "Come on, Marge, you weren't always honest with your kids. No

<hr>

[2]Boston Women's Health Book Collective, *Ourselves and our Children: A Book By and For Parents* (New York: 1978).

one is." I sat and questioned myself and she continued to insist. I couldn't tell her that to my knowledge I always had been. I look back at it now and realize that often it felt like I was losing credibility, but they always grew to understand and learned a little something about being an adult as well. But, yes, we were honest. I think this is one of the three most important factors in raising healthy children and maintaining relationships. Honest communication, with love and trust being the other two. These are survival factors and for sure it's not always easy, but the rewards are great for everyone concerned, and the bonus is that the kids end up sharing their lives with you. It's not too late to start.

> "With unusual patience my father allowed me to follow my dreams and whims during my entire life. When I was ten years old he tried to guide me to a choice between the Latin Gymnasium and the Reasscule: by describing the differences between these schools, he helped me to make my choice as independently as possible. For many long years he very generously supported me financially. In the reorientations of my life he spoke to me as an older friend and never exercised a trace of force on me in important matters. His principles of education were complete trust and the relationship of a friend to me. He knows how grateful I am to him. These lines should be a guide to parents, who try forcibly to turn their children (and those gifted artistically in particular) away from their true careers and thereby make them unhappy."[3]

[3]Wassily Kandinsky, "Reminiscences," *Modern Artists on Art: Ten Unabridged Essays,* by Robert L. Herbert (New Jersey: 1964), p. 20.

To this I would like to add that in my experience with my own children, I approached the relationship very much in this way. I endured criticism from the schools on occasion and other parents because of this liberty. However, my children always seemed to have unaccounted for intelligence and sensibility, each of them in different ways. It surprised me to discover how connected they were at the ages of one and two and then on up. But as adolescents there is an occasional situation where it is difficult. At one of these times when Jennifer was about 14 or 15, I had to take a stand. It was painful to me because so many around me were in such conflict with their children and it was so awful for them. My friend, Gloria, who is a therapist, advised me that there comes a time when you must decide if you are the parent or the friend. I prided myself on being the friend and yet I painfully knew I was the parent, and friend would have to wait for a calmer time. As parent the decision was correct and the friendship was soon resumed with even greater respect. So there are times and there are times. I love what Wassily Kandinsky had to say and for us it worked. Trust is a great gift and rarely does a child wish to risk it. There is great leverage in that knowledge.

The light that came to Lucille Clifton
came in a shift of knowing
when even her fondest sureties
faded away. It was the summer
she understood that she had not understood
and was not mistress even
of her own off eye. Then
the man escaped throwing away his tie and
the children grew legs and started walking
    and
she could see the peril of an
unexamined life.

She closed her eyes, afraid to look for her
authenticity
but the light insists on itself in the world;
a voice from the nondead past started
talking
She closed her ears and it spelled out in her
hand
"You might as well answer the door, my
child
the truth is furiously knocking."[4]

---

[4]Lucille Clifton, *Two Headed Woman* (Massachusetts: 1980).

chapter eleven

# THE YELLOW SCHOOLBUS
## A Private Revelation

One day when I was driving back to the lake where I was staying for six weeks, something happened. I had decided that I needed a break from the family, the meals and the rock and roll. The opportunity opened up for me to move out to Amston Lake where a friend had an empty house. At first, when I quickly said I'd go, I wasn't at all sure. What self-respecting mother leaves her family for six weeks? It took me a matter of seconds before I was sure. Though I was working at the factory full-time, I knew I would well be able to use the mornings, evenings and weekends for some serious solitude. I went gratefully, with a few dollar's worth of simple food and a flannel nightgown. I stared a lot at the reflection of the moon on the frozen lake, tried to ignore the television and the telephone, wrote some poems, sipped some wine at sunset, brewed coffee at sunrise and sang my way to work. Once in a while I had Ron over for a candlelight dinner and it was like a little honeymoon.

Anyway, I was driving back to my hideaway after a long day and there was a yellow schoolbus which had stopped, lights flashing. I waited for the kids to get off and waited some more, but no one got off. I peered through the rear windows and saw a small, sleepy child begin to crawl down off the seat and stagger down the aisle to climb off the bus. She must have been about two feet high and was carrying a small pile of books, a pair of green rubber boots and a Snoopy lunch box. She was sleepy and struggling and exceedingly beautiful in her half awake state. My eyes filled with tears. I didn't know why. Suddenly it triggered a memory for me of the time we lived in Maine and my kids would fall asleep on the schoolbus driving through the mountains and rocky roads toward home. It was a long ride and they were very little and they would fall asleep on the bus in the very same way. It was usually a joy in those days to hear the bus grind to a halt in front of the house, although sometimes it was a startling interruption, with the realization that the day had fled. They would walk up the driveway, three of them through the door into an environment filled with the smell of good things to eat and a feeling of general warmth within.

At that time, I was rather full of myself, very much into being mama, a kind of hip lady. At my age, I really felt that I was something. I had a handle on things. I was weaving tapestries, cooking and baking, canning and freezing, involved in local politics and women's issues and I still turned heads from time to time. Being full of myself, by God, I had an opinion on everything.

But there was an emptiness that was never filled. That I really didn't even recognize as an emptiness at the time. That I just kept filling up with hugs, actions, ideas and wholewheat dinner rolls. Well, now I know what that emptiness was and it was somehow the same thing that was no-thing, the core of myself, the motor that kept me moving through all the misery and joy, through all the boredom and doubt, driving me on in all my blindness, for I didn't recognize the longing or the need to fill the space inside. I didn't even know that I was looking for something but there was always that blind determination to survive long enough to find something "ELSE," something "MORE." Sometimes I'd get a glimmer of what it might be, but I couldn't hold it. It was as evasive as pinching a soft, pink balloon... but I always went along as if I knew there was something going around or over or dumbly through the obstacles to get to the other side. At that time the word "faith" wasn't even in my vocabulary.

So what actually happened that day when I burst into tears behind the schoolbus was that I realized that that period of my life was over. It was indeed another lifetime. It was eons and eons away. I had become a very different person and so had those little people that filled my dreams. Now they are unrecognizably grown, independent and solid. I can breathe a sigh of relief and know that I have a few more answers than I had then. I know that I am at the end of one chapter and the beginning of another. That I will never again be the great, soft, mother earth. I had done it so many times in the past that, of course, I was good at it. I know this because I have learned to see backward. I had been a mother many times, but not always in the same way, because each time was training for the next time around until I got it right. At the same time, it was still a matter of choice, like what course to sign up for this semester.

It's probably attractive to everyone that has a comfortable lifestyle to wish to return over and over again, like keeping ourselves stuck like a needle in a well worn groove, like majoring in our own history without the slightest memory of it. Only until we waken as Soul will this information begin to filter down into mind and then emotion and then the body as soon as we wish to accept and process the data, as fast as we are willing to handle it.

So when I saw that bright yellow schoolbus and the tears came, I knew at once that it was over. That I would probably never again be in that situation. If I do choose to incarnate again into a physical body, it will probably be in a very different role, but there's really no way of knowing at this point. I would not set up a postulate for the future that would limit me in any way. I would hope that I will be open to the dictates of spirit at every given moment, and that too will be my decision as Soul. A great wave of loneliness came over me and sadness. This step I had taken had actually taken me somewhere new. It had moved me from one state of consciousness to another. I was suddenly lifted by a great overwhelming sense of warmth and joy. My love for spirit or spirit's love for me. I didn't know whether I was giving or receiving because that's the way it is with Divine Love. I had let go. I was filled... and the tears continued to fall in a kind of silent ecstasy.

Why is letting go so painful and the result so liberating and fulfilling? I think now as I write this, of the time at Ocean Beach when I was still a scared and skinny kid and I had dared myself to climb the thirty foot diving board for the plunge into the blue-green below. I got to the top, which in itself was a feat, and just stood there, letting all the brave kids somersault and jackknife ahead of me. Finally, I got the courage. I took a deep breath, held my nose and jumped. Time stopped mid-air. I knew there was no turning back and I was glad. I was exultant, filled with pride, adventure and daring with no one to wave to. I had stepped off my secure place alone and made the leap. And that's how it was. The schoolbus episode left me bursting with joy and the new solidity of my eternal self.

Each step of the way up to that point was a lesson of giving and receiving, of learning to stretch and to love, and I had good teachers. We all do, for everyone in our life is given to us to experience, to push us or pull us through our own limitations. It's just a question of continuously adjusting our attitudes within our relationships, communicating with honesty and relating with flexibility.

My husband and children also share in this understanding, and not by accident, for we are each aware that we chose each other to go around with in this possibly last lifetime in a physical body. For each of us it happens by little degrees according to our state of awakeness. This discovering of what we already knew did not happen for us all at once, but rather it was a simultaneous, but individual and sporadic process with very specific and individual discoveries. Of course, these four people I am speaking of are not mine (my husband, my children—only in that we are partners in this twentieth century American life), but we are at the same time each the center of our own universe, each needing to do the things we need to do.

So the yellow schoolbus which for me was once a symbol of fertility, nurturing and togetherness, as it safely delivered my most precious cargo, now for me is a symbol of freedom, spiritual freedom and in a way, it is my destiny like that diving board at Ocean Beach. My challenge is to continue leaping. I will continue at my own pace and there is always another step. Those around me may go faster and farther at times, but it doesn't matter, for it is not a race. What matters to me is that I never stop moving and that every moment counts and that there is no ending and that some of the fastest moving happens sitting down. I may or may not return again into a physical body, but in either case, I will never stop taking the leaps.

In the bathroom mirror
I see
The love you left
on me.

# Independence of Soul

"The attitude of ECKANKAR is the very independence of Soul. Therefore we must cease to cherish opinions of others, the things of this world, and thoughts. The essence, nature, of ECK is hence freedom from all things, not only the attachment to an idea as a factor that conditions the mind and holds Soul in bondage to it, but the simple preference for one idea over another or one opinion over another and for value of one thing or idea rather than the other. All equally enslave Soul to mind, thus chaining the divine, if possible, to the lower aspects of God."[1]

---

[1]Darwin Gross, *Gems of Soul* (California: 1980).

chapter twelve

# THE WAY OUT
## It's Up to You

Jung tells us:

"...since we are dealing with invisible and unknowable things (for God is beyond human understanding, and there is no means of proving immortality), why should we bother about evidence?"... And how do we know that such ideas are not true? Many people would agree with me if I stated flatly that such ideas are probably illusions. What they fail to realize is that the denial is as impossible to "prove" as the assertion of religious belief. We are entirely free to choose which point of view to take."[2]

Jung then goes on to say that this choice is an arbitrary one. I disagree. This choice has to do with the age and unfoldment of Soul.

If we believe, we can move from belief into knowingness. That also cannot be measured or proven. It is at the very least a state of freedom and a state of love, two states of beingness that cannot be described by one person to another. They are two states of beingness that to be known must be experienced, and for this to happen one has to begin with imagination, desire, courage and trust.

The truth of the matter is that there is a way out of the mess we find ourselves in here on this planet, and in these bodies, and everyone is in the same boat

---

[2]Carl G. Jung, *Man and His Symbols* (New York: 1964), pp. 87, 88.

whether it looks that way or not. We can never know the hidden prisons others live in nor the form the prison takes. This is why it is up to us to recognize that the real changes to be made are those we make within. It is not difficult or abstract when one begins to know that the whole purpose of life here on the physical plane is to gain from experience and learn from that experience so that we can return to a higher state of consciousness in this lifetime. It's like going through school and being promoted to the next grade. We continue doing this until we finally catch on that we are truly eternal. We are really Soul and take on new bodies, new personalities each time we incarnate until finally we work our way through mastership of ourselves back to our true home in the heavenly worlds, back to the Godhead. Some think of this goal as reaching Cosmic Consciousness, some as the Source, some as Samadhi, some as pure Energy and some even as in Star Wars as the Force which is very much the way it really is. The big difference being that the negative force isn't so neatly wrapped up in a package as obvious as Darth Vadar. The negative force is much too clever to identify itself so readily and, in actuality, operates on the basis of illusion, much like finding each of our own "Achilles' heels" in order to bring us and keep us down. For this reason we can never get very far through the use of drugs, because drugs are a tool of the negative force.

When we finally begin to become interested in the possibility that there is a dark side and a light side to every moment and that none of us are all dark or all light as long as we remain in a physical body made of matter, we will begin to see with our inner eye. Truth will begin to pour into us as fast as we can handle it, whether we have a religion or not. Truth will find us through a piece of music that lifts Soul, a science fiction story that triggers the imagination, or a fleeting miracle we find hard to ignore...anything to get our inner life functioning, our memory remembering.

There are many teachers out there in the world on all levels and vibrations who can guide us through experiences, help us keep our balance, and give us the teachings we are ready for. Having been with many through other lives and this one, looking for answers to questions that haunted me, questions of existence that we all have, after stumbling in and out of positivity and negativity, I was finally led to the Living ECK Master, whom I was not at all ready to perceive.

I had been hurt before by so called masters/teachers or so I thought. I had been hurt because of the way I had perceived my lessons but I had really gained. Not knowing this, however, I was reluctant to even look at another master. I was looking for a Zen mother. A master with kids, not someone cloistered up in silence somewhere but someone off the street. Someone of this world who knew about bureaucracies and bill collectors.

Hartford began to change. The vibration of where I was living began to soften, to turn sweet. I wondered what was going on and felt good inside hoping the feeling would stay. Then I read that something called Eckankar was having its worldwide seminar at the Civic Center in two weeks. I shrugged. The city grew warmer, friendlier and more alive. Having forgotten about the ad I'd seen, I found myself downtown two weeks later and was drawn into the lobby of the Civic Center. The place was electric. I couldn't leave. A magnet of love held me there as I walked around trying to figure out what was happening. There was a kind of silence while thousands of people of all colors milled. I stood in the center, braless, in patched jeans and an abundance of hair looking at these impeccably straight looking people, trying to comprehend. The art too was a puzzlement. As an artist my intellect didn't approve. The paintings, the sculptures weren't like any I had ever seen. They broke all the rules. Were they art? I couldn't tell, but they did the same thing to me that the people did. They made me high. I floated as if in a dream and couldn't leave this magnet of love.

Africans, Irish, American Indians, Asians, Norwegians, Spanish, Germans and French came and went. There were brochures and books in many languages. Heavenly music blew in from under the closed doors of the coliseum. Baffled, I went home but returned the next day. That night I left my meanderings in the lobby and walked through the door into the coliseum. Seven thousand people sat in silence as Darwin Gross, the Living ECK Master, moved very slowly down the aisles. People were glowing and still as he moved through the crowds shaking hands with his followers. I thought it very corny the way he was preceded by a blue floodlight. I sat in judgment, but always one to grab a little of a good vibration, I thought of getting him to shake my hand. Then I remembered what he'd said on stage: "Give love to those who need it the most." I didn't need it that badly so I dropped the idea. Besides, that blue light was such an obvious prop it was turning me off. He reached my aisle and looked over into my eyes. Without opening his mouth I heard him say from deep within myself, "Take my hand." I reached forward and could see nothing of his face. Blinding light poured from him and I could see no features. I knew then that the blue light was not a prop. It was coming from him, surrounding him and surrounding me.

It took me weeks before my mind could accept what had happened. I had been introduced to a new kind of communication and my travels had begun vividly in the dream state as I was shown many things that changed my life.

Because I am one who values my individuality and

freedom I was reluctant to let go to accept this invitation. It wasn't till weeks later that my mind let loose to the fact that my wish had been granted. That I had found the one who could lead me to mastership of myself. I had found my "zen mother" and more, much more, because through him I am learning the skills I need to deal with my life, not a monastic life but the life of a twentieth century American woman. For four years now I have been working my way toward mastership. Adventure after adventure, challenge after challenge, in training for the mastership that is bringing me first to Self-Realization and second to God-Realization. The thing is that in this training process one experiences moments of Self-Realization and even God-Realization, so it isn't some far away abstract goal I'm heading for. It is right here and now and the mastership itself is the ability to KEEP it in the here and now while living any lifestyle one may choose.

Mainly, it isn't like trying desperately to give up all negativity, desperately trying to become pure in order to have the ecstatic state in order to have God. It isn't like an impossible dream, a far away goal. It is more like an organic process. When one's attention is on giving, that in itself is a purification process. When one is willing to let go of certain attachments, they will begin to disappear painlessly. Until then, it doesn't matter. There is no guilt involved when a person sincerely desires to serve God but can't seem to give up certain habits. One doesn't have to wait until they become pure to give to God. We become pure by giving to God. It just happens that way, that is the process.

Your destiny is within your hands to direct or be directed by. It is for you to choose. There are so many wise beings walking this planet and beyond. There is a teacher for each of us. If you don't know where to begin to find yours, ask. Find a word that will raise your vibration. Chant it, and with your love for yourself and your love for your universe, make it sacred. Sing it whether it be Darwin or Jesus or Trees or Please, whether it's a sound from a cello or a flute you wish to recall, dwell in that sound until you are lifted and ask for what it is you want. This should not be done with intense concentration or determination but with gentleness and detachment.

It will not be difficult if we are sincere in reaching for the truth and willing to step onto unknown ground. If we do this with logic and reason or great expectations we will not get very far, for the result, real as it is, is often very subtle. Too subtle for our stubborn minds to recognize what is happening. But if we open up and let the mind do its cartwheels and bellydances till it's tired of entertaining us and then relax with some deep breaths looking into the now blank screen of the mind with the desire for reaching our highest selves, we will become the knower. It probably won't happen right away but if we keep at it, it will happen without fail!

How do I know? It's simple. I just do. When you know you know, but I can't prove it. I'm not asking you to believe me either. I'm just giving it to you to try for yourself, to prove it to yourself. You can do it.

If you look back you will remember that you too have had things happen that were so intense you could never really communicate it. Or something funny—you'd try to explain and it wouldn't draw much response, and you'd laugh saying, "you had to be there." You knew it was funny but you sure couldn't prove it.

No matter what, just know that whatever way you are going and wherever you are going, you are doing it because there's something in it for you to learn. When you start to get restless, then it's time to take the next step, and no matter where you are there's always another step. For you too are Soul, and you too are working your way back home.

THE TRUTH IN THESE PAGES IS OF THE HERE AND THE NOW THROUGH THE CURRENT CONSCIOUSNESS OF MYSELF AND IS SUBJECT TO CHANGE WITHOUT FURTHER NOTICE. TRUTH, THEREFORE, IS YOURS TO FIND FROM WITHIN YOUR OWN TRUE SELF, MOMENT BY MOMENT AND WITH LOVE.

# BIBLIOGRAPHY

Albers, Anni, *On Designing*. Connecticut: Wesleyan University, 1943.

Alpert, Richard, Dr., *Be Here Now*. New Mexico: Lama Foundation, 1971.

Bird, Caroline and McKay, David, *Everything a Woman Needs to Know to Get Paid What She's Worth*. New York: Bantam, 1981.

Boston Womens Health Book Collective, *Ourselves and Our Children, A Book by and for Parents*. New York: Random House, 1978.

Castaneda, Carlos, *Teachings of Don Juan, a Yaqui Way of Knowledge*. New York: Pocket Books, Inc., 1968.

Chicago, Judy, *Through the Flower*. New York: Doubleday, 1975.

Clifton, Lucille, *Two Headed Woman*. Massachusetts: University of Massachusetts, 1980.

Dowling, Colette, *Cinderella Complex*. New York: Summit Books, 1981.

Fiska, Heidi and Zehring, Karen, *How to Start your Own Business*. Mississippi: March, 1979.

Franck, Frederick, *The Zen of Seeing*. New York: Random House, 1973.

Graber, Anya Foos, *Skycleaver*. Connecticut: Thadian Publications, 1975.

Gross, Darwin, *Gems of Soul*. California: IWP Publishing, 1980.

Gross, Darwin, *Your Right to Know*. California: IWP Publishing, 1979.

Herbert, Robert L, *Modern Artists on Art: Ten Unabridged Essays*. New Jersey: Prentice-Hall, Inc., 1964.

Jaffe, Hans L. and A. Busignani editors, *Klee*. New York: Crown Publishers, Twentieth Century Masters Series, 1972.

Jung, Carl G., *Man and His Symbols*. New York: Doubleday, 1964.

*Kahlil Gibran Diary for 1980*. Alfred A. Knopf.

Levertov-Goodman, Denise, *O Taste and See*. New York: New Directions Publishing Corp., 1964.

Plath, Sylvia, *The Bell Jar*. New York: Har-Row, 1971.

Reps, *Gold Fish Signatures*. Vermont: Charles E. Tuttle Co. Publishers, 1969.

Richards, M. C., *Centering*. Connecticut: Wesleyan University Press, 1962.

Rilke, Rainer Maria, *Letters to a Young Poet*. New York: Norton, 1963.

Scott, Niki, *The Working Woman: A Handbook*. Kansas: Andrews and McNeal, 1977.

Shapiro, Joan, *Coloring Book*. Connecticut: Blue Spruce Press, 1978.

Sheehy, Gail, *Passages*. New York: Bantam, 1977.

Shelton, Herbert, *Food Combining Made Easy*. Texas: Dr. Shelton Health School, 1951.

Siegel, Ronald K., "Accounting for After Life Experiences." *Psychology Today,* January 1981.

Simon, Linda, *The Biography of Alice B. Toklas*. New York: Hearst Corp., 1967.

Steinem, Gloria, "Why Women Work," *Ms. Magazine,* March 1979.

Stevens, Barry and John, *Embrace Tiger, Return to Mountain*. (introduction) Utah: Real People Press, 1973.

Swenson, May, *New And Selected Things Taking Place.* Massachusetts: Little, Brown and Company, 1978.

Truppin, Michael and Berman, Alvin, *Harpers Bazaar.* New York: March 1981.

Twitchell, Paul, *Anitya.* California: IWP Publishing.

Twitchell, Paul, *ECKANKAR Dictionary.* California: IWP Publishing, 1973.

Twitchell, Paul, *Herbs, the Magic Healers.* California: IWP Publishing, 1971.

Waniek, Marilyn Nelson, *Bali Hai Calls Mama.*

Watts, Alan, *Does it Matter?* Essays on Man's Relation to Materiality. New York: Vintage Books edition of Random House, 1971.

Whitman, Walt, *Leaves of Grass.*

Suggested introductory books published by IWP
on ECKANKAR, the most ancient spiritual
teaching in all the universes . . .

IN MY SOUL I AM FREE
(Biography on Sri Paul Twitchell by Brad Steiger)

YOUR RIGHT TO KNOW
(Compilation of articles on contemporary subjects)

THE TIGER'S FANG
(An understanding of levels of heaven)

THE FLUTE OF GOD (Psychology of Spirit)

THE SPIRITUAL NOTEBOOK
(History of ECKANKAR)

STRANGER BY THE RIVER
(Love and wisdom of the ages)

LETTERS TO GAIL, VOLS. I & II
(Basic text)

FROM HEAVEN TO THE PRAIRIE
(Biography of Sri Darwin Gross)

THE WIND OF CHANGE
(Humorous recollections of Sri Harold Klemp)


Books on ECKANKAR can be found or ordered at your
local bookstore.

In many areas around the world, discussion classes on the
introductory books of ECKANKAR are being held, which
the public is welcome to attend. ECKANKAR Centers will
be listed in the local telephone book. For a free book catalog,
more information on ECKANKAR and/or ECKANKAR
activities, please write to:

**ECKANKAR**
**P.O. Box 3100**
**Menlo Park, CA 94025 U.S.A.**

# BOOK ORDER COUPON

*Mail to:*

**ECKANKAR**
P.O. Box 3100
Menlo Park, CA 94025 U.S.A.

☐ Please send me a free book catalog.

I enclose $_____ for the book(s) checked below.

International Orders: Please remit Int'l Money Order
or check payable in U.S. funds to ECKANKAR.

QTY

| | | |
|---|---|---|
| _____ | 0104 | **In My Soul I Am Free** $2.95 |
| _____ | 0106 | **The Tiger's Fang** $2.50 papbk |
| _____ | 010699 | **The Tiger's Fang** $8.95 hb |
| _____ | 0110 | **Your Right to Know** $1.95 papbk |
| _____ | 011099 | **Your Right to Know** $8.95 hb |
| _____ | 011299 | **From Heaven to the Prairie** $14.95 hb |
| _____ | 0126 | **The Flute of God** $2.95 |
| _____ | 0128 | **The Spiritual Notebook** $2.95 |
| _____ | 0132 | **Stranger by the River** $5.95 |
| _____ | 0154 | **Letters to Gail, Vol. I** $5.95 papbk |
| _____ | 0155 | **Letters to Gail, Vol. II** $9.95 hb |
| _____ | 0188 | **The Wind of Change** $3.95 papbk |
| _____ | 018899 | **The Wind of Change** $6.95 hb |

Total $_____

6% sales tax (California only) $_____

Add 10% for shipping $_____
**75¢ minimum**

TOTAL ENCLOSED $_____

Name _____
(please print)

Street _____

City _____ State_____

Country _____ Postal Code_____

194

*(detach here)*

**Є-K**

☐ Please send me more information on ECKANKAR.

☐ I am interested in information on discussion or study groups in my area.

*Mail to:*

**ECKANKAR**
**P.O. Box 3100**
**Menlo Park, CA 94025**
**U.S.A.**

*detach here*

Name _____

Street _____

City_____ State _____

Country _____ Zip _____

186